Praise for *The Officer's Daughter*

"*The Officer's Daughter*, by Elle Johnson, is a masterpiece. More than that, it's the perfect book for our troubled time. Johnson has written the deepest, most emotionally resonant understanding of forgiveness and justice I have ever read."
—Darin Strauss, bestselling author of *Half a Life*

"Immensely moving." —*New York Times*

"A powerful portrait of one family's 'grief that will never end.'"
—*People*

"This fierce, probing memoir beautifully explores the powerful aftershocks of staggering loss. How does a family go on, after senseless, random violence claims one of their own? Buried secrets fester until someone is brave enough to go digging. Elle Johnson has written a gift of a book—one that instructs and inspires, even as it breaks your heart."
—Dani Shapiro, *New York Times* bestselling author of *Inheritance*

"*The Officer's Daughter* is a powerful dissertation on the legacy of violence; a telling journey to the place in the heart where forgiveness is found. Elle Johnson's words are beautiful, poignant and painful; and always deeply resonant with truth. This book has an echo that stays with you well after you have turned the last page."
—*New York Times* bestselling author Michael Connelly

"Screen writer Johnson debuts with a beautiful and emotional memoir of a family tragedy. . . . This searing story deserves a wide readership."
—*Publishers Weekly* (starred review)

"Powerful reflections on crime, murder, punishment, and redemption . . . A remarkable exploration of forgiveness by a veteran storyteller." —*Kirkus Reviews* (starred review)

THE OFFICER'S DAUGHTER

A Memoir of Family and Forgiveness

Elle Johnson

HARPER

NEW YORK • LONDON • TORONTO • SYDNEY

HARPER

A hardcover edition of this book was published in 2021 by HarperCollins Publishers.

HarperCollins books may be purchased for educational, business, or sales promotional use. For information, please email the Special Markets Department at SPsales@harpercollins.com.

FIRST HARPER PAPERBACKS EDITION PUBLISHED 2022.

Designed by Bonni Leon-Berman

Library of Congress Cataloging-in-Publication Data has been applied for.

ISBN 978-0-06-301133-5 (pbk.)

22 23 24 25 26 LSC 10 9 8 7 6 5 4 3 2 1

For my mother, who didn't want me to write this.

Forgive me.

THE OFFICER'S DAUGHTER

CHAPTER ONE

When I was sixteen, my sixteen-year-old cousin, Karen, had her face blown off at point-blank range by a sawed-off shotgun in a robbery gone awry at a local Burger King in the Bronx. It was early Saturday morning, April 4, 1981. Karen's father was a homicide detective. My father was a parole officer. They joined more than fifty NYPD officers and the FBI to help track down the killers in a cross-country manhunt that lasted two weeks. For two weeks Karen's murder was covered by the local New York news. For two weeks I was spinning from the shock. This was my loss of innocence, the moment in my childhood when I understood that the world didn't work the way my parents said it did. After Karen was killed, I questioned everything and everyone—especially my father.

More than three decades later, I hadn't stopped thinking about Karen's murder. Though I had left the middle-class Black enclave of Hollis, Queens, where I grew up and relocated to Los Angeles, the trauma of that event followed me. I thought about it on her birthday and mine. At Thanksgiving and Christmas. On the anniversaries of the day she was killed and the day the killers were finally caught. And on the day Karen was buried, which also happened to be my father's birthday. The events of Karen's murder played in my mind on an endless loop, like an old record on repeat. I retold the story so frequently that I had developed a script I could recite easily, without betraying the depth of emotion buried beneath the fluid, familiar phrasing: "When I was sixteen, my sixteen-year-old cousin, Karen, had her face blown off at point-blank range by a sawed-off shotgun in a robbery gone awry at a local Burger King in the Bronx."

One morning in September 2014, I got up early to write. I was sitting in my house in LA, a cozy Spanish-style bungalow built in 1926, a time when my neighborhood was still orange groves connected by dirt roads. The front was all east-facing french doors and arched windows that let in brilliant morning light. I was reading emails. Procrastinating before getting to work, when I saw a message from my cousin Warren, Karen's older brother.

Karen's killer was up for parole.

Warren asked me to write a letter encouraging the parole board not to set his sister's killer free. Warren had never asked me to do anything like this before, so his email took me by surprise.

I had seen Warren two months earlier at a family gathering back in New York. He hadn't mentioned the upcoming parole hearing. I thought maybe the nature of the occasion had precluded such talk. It was a memorial service for my favorite uncle, who was eighty-two years old when he died. Rather than mourning a death, we were celebrating a full, complex, and rewarding life. Warren was at the memorial along with his younger brother, Geoffrey, and their mother, my aunt Barbara. Every time I saw the Marsh family I thought of Karen. The family resemblance was so strong—light skin, light eyes, bright, open faces—that I could easily imagine what Karen would have looked like today. But we never talked about Karen or her murder. It was as though she had never existed.

That night, as we caught up with small talk and told tall tales about our dearly departed uncle and the family, Karen's absence lingered like a rainstorm. When I breathed in, misty images of Karen and me came to mind: whispering about boys; giggling as we sneaked extra sweets out of Grandma's crystal candy dish; wearing the matching cartoon geisha nightgowns she'd given me at my birthday slumber party, then braiding our hair the same way to look like twins. But then I flashed on a photograph—the black-and-white close-up of a smiling Karen from her funeral program. I wanted to ask Warren and Aunt Barbara if they remembered it the way I did. I wanted to know how they had carried the weight of Karen's murder through the years. I wanted to guess what Karen's life would have been like had she lived: happily married with children, like her brothers; divorced and dating, following her dreams, like me. I wondered if Warren and Aunt Barbara knew that Karen's murder was a pivotal event that had shaped my adolescent life and beyond.

Back home in Los Angeles, I pulled a box of keepsakes from the closet and shuffled through it, looking for mementos of Karen. There were only two. The first was a copy of her funeral program. The picture of Karen showed her younger than I remembered. Her hair was pulled back away from her face. She looked like she was in elementary school. The second memento was an eight-by-ten color photo of Karen and me at my sweet sixteen.

In the photograph, we are standing next to each other. Her arm is around my waist. My hand clutches her shoulder like a needy claw. She wears velvet pants in her favorite color—purple—a satiny cream-colored rodeo shirt, and a beige ten-gallon hat. Her curly dark bangs cover her forehead like wild mushrooms sprouting in a meadow. She has a tomboy's cocky swagger.

My shoulders are stooped and remind me of how uncomfortable I was in my own skin back then. I wear a black polyester jumpsuit with a halter top held up by spaghetti straps. The satiny fabric drapes around my waist and tapers at the ankles. A turquoise sash hangs awkwardly from my hips. My face has the look of ecstatic exhaustion. I remember how happy I was that night.

I had never heard of a sweet sixteen before my junior year and didn't know I wanted one until Karen and all the girls in my class started having them. My sweet sixteen was held in the community room of a church off Queens Boulevard and was catered by my father's friend who was a fireman and knew that the least expensive way to feed a bunch of teenagers was with twelve-foot-long sub sandwiches and a vanilla sheet cake slathered with buttercream icing. My mother found a DJ, who played everything from Afrika Bambaataa's "Planet Rock" to "Rock Lobster" by the B-52's. I invited everyone in my class and danced until my long, straightened hair frizzed up into loose curls and the turquoise sash around my waist darkened with sweat. I spent the evening with one eye on the door, waiting for Karen to show up.

I desperately wanted Karen to be there. I wanted everyone to see me with my beautiful, cool cousin, who would make me cooler by association. The party was almost over when she arrived with Aunt Barbara. Karen's cowboy hat drew looks; the sparkle of her green eyes got people who were ready to leave back on the dance floor. When she stopped to take a break, I stood with her on the sidelines, talking and laughing, until Cameron sidled up to us. Cameron was the first boy in three years to have asked me on a date. He'd taken me out on the bus, made out with me behind a mortuary, then dumped me over the phone, all in the same weekend. In the ultimate show of teenage-girl insecurity, I'd invited him to my party. He flirted shamelessly with Karen, but Karen made a point of ignoring him to talk to me. Undeterred, Cameron whispered in my ear, "I'm in love with your cousin. You think she'd go out with me?" Instead of anger, disappointment, or envy, I felt pride. When I told Karen what Cameron had said, she said, "Never," threw her arm around my waist, and pulled me away. Then my mother took our picture.

We're both smiling. Karen's lips are pressed closed, her cheeks are rounded and high. She looks delighted with herself, mischievous—like she has a secret. Looking at the photo, I remember that I had a secret, too. I was sure that from then on Karen and I were going to be best friends.

That was the last time I saw her. She was killed three months later.

I TOOK THE PICTURE of Karen and me at my sweet sixteen and tacked it up next to the email from my cousin Warren on the bulletin board above my desk. Unsettled, I wandered to the front of my house. It was still dark out. The blue blush of first light had not yet edged out the darkness. Everything was black. Usually this stillness before dawn was my favorite time of day. My mind was open, my thoughts unburdened. I felt like I was stealing time. I took comfort in knowing that the world outside my windows was still shrouded by night. Growing up, I was afraid of the dark, but as I became an adult, it seemed the darkness protected me from a harsh light.

I sat down at the dining room table and opened my laptop to write. I couldn't concentrate. I made my living writing police procedurals for television. My job was to tell stories about cops, crimes, and criminals. I had written television episodes loosely based on Karen's murder: the shooting, the investigation afterward, and my father's part in the manhunt that ensued. That morning, I realized I had never really looked closely at what Karen's murder had done to my family, to me, to my relationship with my father—who had loomed large in my adolescent life.

I wanted to honor Warren's request to write to the parole board, but I didn't know where to begin. Or what I wanted to say. I would have asked my father, the former parole officer, for guidance, but he had died in 2005. Maybe my letter to the parole board should explain how Santiago Ramirez had deprived me of not just a cousin but also a best friend. I realized that all these years, whenever I thought about Karen, I focused only on her death and the events surrounding her murder. Before I could write anything, I had to throw away the script I'd come to rely on, unpack the memories I had neatly boxed up, and unwrap the emotions I kept under control. I needed to allow myself to feel everything again. I needed to remember how Karen had lived.

CHAPTER TWO

October 16, 1980

Karen sauntered into her own sweet sixteen party a full hour and a half after her guests were told to arrive. There must have been three hundred people crammed into the community room in the basement of a Bronx apartment building.

Waiting.

Being from Queens, I didn't know what to expect from a party in the "boogie down Bronx." Not that I had been to so many parties in my own neighborhood. The invitation had been addressed to the whole family, but I'd assumed it was really meant for me. I didn't know how to drive, and even if I could have figured out how to get there by subway or bus, my parents never would have let me make a trip to that neighborhood. Or any neighborhood. At night. On my own.

I was glad my parents were with me.

When we pulled up, my father leaned close to the steering wheel, then looked out the windshield and up at the twenty-story apartment building where Karen's party was being held. He sucked his teeth, then laughed.

"Man, would you look at this," he said.

An overflowing trash can sat next to the graffiti-covered walls of the building. Broken concrete walkways cut through islands of dirt and dead brown grass surrounded by stray garbage—trampled scraps of paper, ripped plastic wrappers, a used diaper.

He backed up into a red zone and parked the car illegally. Then he reached into the glove compartment and took out a placard from the parole department. It was supposed to be for official business, but he placed it on the dash.

"Ricky, do you think this neighborhood is safe?" my mother asked.

"No. But we're here now." My father chuckled, then walked around the car to open the door for my mother.

"I don't understand. Why would they have it someplace like this?" My mother looked up at my father, then held his hand as she stepped out into the cool October night. She took a quick look up and down the street, then secured her purse strap over her arm and pulled the fur collar of her wool coat close around her neck.

"Well, Warren said it only cost him twenty dollars to reserve the room."

I slid out across the back seat, holding the purple Macy's sweater my mother had wrapped up as a gift. We started to walk toward the building when my father stopped us.

"Wait a minute, wait a minute. Let me put on my coat."

My father adjusted the Windsor knot on his tie, buttoned his navy blue suit jacket, then reached across the front seat for his gunmetal gray wool coat. He unfolded it slowly, shaking it out like a matador might unfurl his cape to draw a bull out into the open.

I followed his gaze as his eyes shifted, scanning the block the way he was trained to as a parole officer, taking in the local characters—a homeless man lying on the bus bench, an older woman struggling under the weight of her grocery bags, a pack of boys roaming the streets, looking for trouble.

"Wait here." My father walked across the street to a cluster of young Black men leaning against a parked car like crows on a wire. They smoked cigarettes and took swigs from the mouth of an open bottle hidden in a brown paper bag. They wore dark tracksuits and white sneakers, Kangol hats at an angle with gold chains dripping straight down their chests. One had on a pair of sunglasses. They stopped talking and turned to look at my father as he swaggered into their midst. The brown paper bag disappeared.

The young men stood up and leaned in to listen. They started laughing.

My father grinned, took out a cigarette, tapped it on the pack. Sunglasses stepped up with a match and lit it for him. He blew out the smoke right into their circle.

"Oh, come on, Ricky," my mother said. "It's cold out here."

She'd seen my father's act before—the Jedi mind trick of quiet coercion through charming intimidation. My father turned and pointed to our car, then watched the young men's faces: not a one dared even glance at me or my mother. They nodded their acceptance of a very important mission—to make sure nothing happened to our car. My father put the cigarette between his teeth and shook Sunglasses's hand before walking back toward us.

"It's this way." My father held my mother's hand and led us to the dark back side of the building. I could hear Grandmaster Flash rapping "The Message."

"Broken glass, everywhere / people pissing on the stairs, you know they just don't care."

We walked down a poorly lit concrete ramp to a door with

a construction paper sign taped to it. KAREN'S SWEET 16 was written out in purple marker and outlined with glitter.

We stepped into a large open room. Inside, it was dark and hard to see, but it felt crowded. Clusters of people stood close to the walls, facing the empty middle of the floor, where red, blue, and yellow lights flashed to the beat from two vertical towers on both sides of the DJ's table.

A cracked linoleum floor sprouted concrete pillars that held up a low chessboard-tiled ceiling with exposed fluorescent light bulbs. It was an ugly space that Karen and my aunt had tried to dress up. The decorations reminded me of Karen's frilly bedroom. Purple and white crepe paper streamers hung like cumulus clouds from the ceiling. Hand-size purple and white balloons drifted like fog across the floor. Aunt Barbara was in a corner fussing with the tablecloth covering a folding card table full of gifts.

"Hi. Hi. Hello," she said, kissing each of us on the cheek, her hand squeezing each shoulder.

I handed Aunt Barbara the gift.

"You look so pretty," she said, holding my coat open to get a look at the dress.

"Lord and Taylor," my mother said. "My friend Mrs. Wilson gave it to us. It used to be Valerie's, her middle girl." I wished my mother wouldn't announce it every time our clothes were not our own. But I think she felt it was lying, like we were trying to be something that we were not.

"Well, it certainly looks good on you," Aunt Barbara said.

Aunt Barbara was one of my favorite relatives. Soft-spoken and kind. Dependable. She was small, with a child's round, cookie dough–colored face, hidden by glasses, framed by curly hair. She smiled easily and often. It was hard to imagine her as a probation officer, carrying a gun, wearing a bulletproof vest to work. Or determining the fate of convicted criminals by reinvestigating their crimes after trial and writing the judges' sentencing recommendations.

"This is some neighborhood you picked," my father said.

"But it looks so nice down here," my mother quickly countered. "I like the balloons. And the streamers. Very pretty."

Aunt Barbara smiled and pointed behind the DJ table. "You see them?"

Two linebacker-size men in NYPD windbreakers stood against the wall with their arms at their sides. I recognized the bulge beneath their left armpits where their guns were holstered.

"I don't think we'll have any problems tonight," she said.

My father clasped his hands behind his back. "No, no. I don't expect that we will."

I watched Aunt Barbara do a quick scan of my father's upper body. Her eyes dropped down to his ankles and the brown leather holster holding a snub-nosed .38-caliber Colt beneath his left pant leg.

"Richard, did you bring a gun to my daughter's sweet sixteen?" Aunt Barbara teased.

"Didn't you?" my father shot back.

She shrugged. "Warren has his."

My mother harrumphed. "With all these guns, I hope no one gets shot."

The kitchen door swung open. A bright light cut across the room. Through a hazy white curtain of cigarette smoke I saw more adults—older relatives, Aunt Barbara's neighbors and family friends—standing around, laughing and talking like it was Easter brunch or Christmas dinner.

"Go on in and make yourselves a plate," Aunt Barbara said. "We're not putting the food out until Karen gets here."

"Where is Karen?" I asked.

"She'll be here. She's coming. You go enjoy yourself." Aunt Barbara nodded me toward the flashing lights on the dance floor as she and my parents headed the other way and disappeared into the kitchen, where the grown-ups were.

I pretended to inspect the gifts. I picked them up, shook the small ones close to my ear, restacking them by size, but really I was checking out the room, looking for familiar faces, like the girls from Karen's sleepover when we were thirteen. We'd spread out on sleeping bags and blankets on her parents' living room floor. We ate pizza in our pajamas and played truth or dare until one girl started crying and the room divided into school cliques I didn't understand. Karen didn't sleep in a sleeping bag on the floor. Even if her guests had to. And when lights-out came, I got to sleep with Karen in her room in a trundle next to her big four-poster canopy bed. We stayed up past the point of exhaustion into delirium and talked about nothing while laughing at everything until Aunt Barbara rapped on the wall and told us to settle down and go to sleep.

Looking around the sweet sixteen, I didn't see any of Karen's friends from the sleepover. The room was full of Black faces, and all those girls had been white. My parents would be happy. Whenever they picked me up from a party they always wanted to know the race of every kid at the event. I'd always say "Human," annoyed that they cared how many Black kids were there besides me. Especially when they knew the answer was almost always that I was the only one.

My parents sent my sister and me to a Lutheran elementary

school where we were surrounded by blond-haired, blue-eyed Germans. Then my mother used her standing as a teacher and pulled strings to avoid the crime-ridden, all-Black public high school nearest our house. We ended up at Jamaica High, a racially diverse school, except in the honors classes, where most of the kids were white and predominantly Jewish and my sister and I were once again the only Blacks.

I was used to being an anomaly at school and then singled out by the Black kids on my block when I was in elementary school. Pelted with rocks, sometimes bricks, at the instigation of one family down the street. It stopped only when my father paid the parents a visit in his official capacity as a law enforcement officer investigating what he labeled criminal assaults against his daughter that might end with an unofficial ass kicking if the attacks didn't stop. In high school I was tall enough to not get beaten up. The sticks and stones turned into words that were no less hurtful. Name-calling and insults hurled at me from across the street or down the aisle of a bus that disparaged me for being light, talking white, and acting like "you think you so cute."

I squinted into the darkness at Karen's guests and wondered how Karen had managed to make so many Black friends.

I thought, *This is my chance.*

If the Black girls at the party could be friends with Karen, maybe they could be my friends, too. After all, Karen was even lighter than I was. So light she could pass for white. She still went to an all-white Catholic high school for girls and wore a uniform every day. She was also bound by the rules of a law enforcement household much stricter than mine, because both her parents were "on the job."

Uncle Warren was a homicide detective in Manhattan who

wore his gun nestled close to his heart and within easy drawing distance of his right hand. His shoulder holster had thick brown leather straps that lay across his wide back and barrel chest like a warning. Karen's parents demanded good grades and blind obedience, just like mine. And just like mine, Karen's parents ensured their daughter's safe passage in a world they knew all too well to be dangerous and full of heinous, vile people—suspects and convicted criminals—by escorting her everywhere.

Except Karen's parents had let her get a job. She was going to spend the summer studying Spanish in Madrid. It was an adventure my mother, a high school Spanish teacher, couldn't stop talking about. To help pay for the trip and sock away some extra spending cash, Karen had just started working a night shift at the local Burger King. Getting a job was something my father simply would not allow. "You're going to be working for the rest of your life," my father said. "You don't have to start now." He made it seem like it was for our benefit, but really he didn't want us out in the world, out of his sight and control. Making our own money meant we wouldn't need him to buy things for us.

At the party I clung to the wall, walking outside clusters of party guests who had migrated into the middle of the room. Everyone seemed to know one another. No one was standing alone. I pulled my mouth into a close-lipped smile and looked for an opening, the smallest of spaces between friends that I could slip into without drawing attention and still slide naturally into the conversation.

"Hi, hello, hey," I said in a voice barely loud enough to hear as I strolled behind groups of friends. That was as far as I got. I was greeted with a confused smile—*Who are you and why are you talking to me?*—or a dismissive head nod before the guests turned back to their conversations. I preferred that to the once-over I got from some of the other girls. It was an eye-rolling bat of their eyelashes that started at my ungainly large feet and moved in what felt like slow motion up to the relaxed straight-like-a-white-girl hair on my head.

They were confident in their inexpensive yet trendy outfits. The kind you'd buy from storefront shops on crowded avenues under the el train. Their hair was styled into geometric shapes, pressed against their scalps in waves or rows of hot-pressed curls that stayed perfectly in place, defying gravity.

They wore gold jewelry that spelled out their names or other synonyms for who they were, like SASSY, SEXY, or simply TROUBLE. Their fingernails were long talons with polish and designs on the tips. They wore makeup. They had boyfriends. They went out at night. They carried knockoff designer handbags with lipstick and Life Savers, loose little rectangles of Bazooka Joe chewing gum and square packets of condoms tucked inside faux reptile-skin wallets.

No one was getting close enough to me to care how my lips looked or what my breath smelled like. I never carried money. My parents still paid for everything. I didn't have a set of keys to my own home. My parents were always there to let me in.

I saw my cousin Warren Jr. and decided to follow him. Warren was just as striking as Karen—light eyes, light skin. He wore his hair in a big black Afro that drooped under its own weight. He dashed around the party, from group to group, shaking hands and smiling, giving hugs, then running off. I shuffled alongside a conga line of adoring girls who trailed behind him.

He did a double take when he finally noticed me. He wrapped his arms around me, squeezed my shoulders like a python, and lifted my feet off the ground. "How you doing, cuz?" he asked, kissing my hair.

He walked away before I could answer.

I smiled at the girls following him, then retreated to a long folding table with bowls of chips and a rubber tub full of soda cans covered in ice. I put a handful of chips in a napkin, then rummaged through the ice for a can of cold cola. I tried to come up with topics of conversation. Things I might have in common with Karen's Black friends. But as I went down the list of my activities in my head, everything sounded so dull.

Homework. Reading. Studying at the library.

Sometimes I wasn't even studying. Instead, I wandered the shelves, looking for interesting books to read about things I wanted to know or thought I should know.

I taught myself how to type ninety words a minute. I learned the alphabet to American Sign Language—what if I met a Deaf person one day? I practiced the flute. Rehearsed for the school play. Or worked on a scene for my theater class downtown once a week.

I was in before dark. I ate dinner with my parents at the kitchen table every night. I watched television with them, too. The only thing I could think of to say was *Hi, I'm Karen's cousin.*

"Hi. You're Karen's cousin," a voice behind me said.

I turned and saw David. He stuffed a chip into his mouth, then held out his hand for me to shake. "I don't know if you remember, I met you at Karen's house."

David was my height, white with tousled sandy hair and a line of freckles across his nose. His hands and arms were like the chiseled marble of his namesake sculpted by Michelangelo. Yes, I remembered David.

As I shook his hand my shoulders relaxed—I didn't realize I had been holding them up around my earlobes all night. I let out a breath and felt lighter. I was grateful for the company and tired of holding out a smile with no one to receive it.

"Are you here with anyone?" David moved closer to me.

"My parents," I said, then clarified: "My sister's away at college."

David leaned over to scoop up a fistful of chips and offered me some. Thoughts that had been trapped in the back of my mind gushed out of my mouth like rainwater through a downspout. I went on about classes and college, studying for the SATs, Karen was going to Spain but I had my eye on a summer internship at the Metropolitan Museum of Art, in the medieval art collection at the Cloisters museum in Upper Manhattan, which would be my first job of any kind and I hoped my parents would let me do it.

"Why wouldn't they?" he asked. "I mean, it sounds kinda like school anyways."

I shrugged—I didn't want to admit how controlled I was by my parents—then blurted out, "I love school."

David lifted an eyebrow. I laughed nervously, worried that he would think I was strange. But then he laughed with me.

It was easy for me to talk to David. He nodded through mouthfuls of chips and was polite enough to pretend to be interested in what I was saying. He smiled sheepishly when I caught him looking over my shoulder, eyes searching around the dark room. "Do you know people here?" I asked.

"Just Karen. Wonder where she is."

"Still getting dressed, probably."

David smiled to himself.

I got the feeling he was hoping for something more from Karen than casual friendship. David recognized someone on the other side of the room and excused himself. I watched him disappear into the crowd, then I wandered into the bright light of the kitchen, where the adults were eating. I slipped into a space next to my mother, who was sitting at one of the tables. She was leaning over, shielding her dress with a napkin that she held under her chin up against her chest. She carefully forked up mouthfuls of collard greens, black-eyed peas, and chicken from the partitions of a paper plate.

"Leave it to you to find the only white person in the room to talk to," she said between bites.

Heat rose in my cheeks. I turned away, stung, and looked around the kitchen.

After a moment she squeezed my arm, then shook it. "You want something to eat? Why don't you get something?"

"I'm not hungry," I lied, pulling away.

I moved across the room to stand closer to my father. He was seated in a folding chair at the head of a long table. He leaned back with his legs crossed and a cigarette trailing smoke from his hand resting on his thigh.

The men around him were laughing. I could tell by the way they looked at one another—for support or confirmation—that my father had said something outrageous or controversial, inappropriate or even offensive. The men were laughing, but they weren't having fun.

It was laughter born of shock. The kind of laugh that puts distance between you and what was said and the speaker. It made me anxious.

My father leaned over and twirled the tip of his cigarette

around the bottom of a ceramic ashtray on the table. "It's true. You may not want to believe it, you may not like it." He let the words hang in the air while he put the cigarette to his lips and took a long pull, then blew out a stream of white smoke. "But that's the way it is, baby."

The men laughed again. At my father's stubbornness and defiance. What else could they do? Especially if the topic was politics or racism—two of my father's favorite subjects. Laughing was the only way to avoid an argument, to engage without agreeing.

Disagreeing with my father meant starting a conversation that would not end until he had convinced you otherwise. My father would take whatever the topic was and bring it up every time he saw you, over and over until he understood your misguided position or had hammered his points into your brain and convinced you that you were wrong. Those who didn't know this proceeded at their peril. Arguing a point successfully only made you the sought-after expert on that particular subject in my father's eyes. Either way, you were on his radar—and that was not somewhere you wanted to be.

For once I was glad to be left out of the conversation.

I leaned back into a corner of the wall. That's when the DJ started to play Stevie Wonder's "Happy Birthday." It was a pop song with an unmistakable hook. "*Happy birthday to ya, / happy birthday to ya, / happy biiiirth day.*" Unrelentingly upbeat, it was actually a protest song written to garner support for a national holiday to celebrate the birthday of the slain civil rights leader Martin Luther King Jr., shot dead on the balcony of the Lorraine Motel in Memphis, Tennessee, on April 4, 1968.

I just never understood
How a man who died for good
Could not have a day that would
Be set aside for his recognition.

The song would turn into a much-loved, alternative birthday song for Black people, similar to how "Lift Every Voice and Sing" is considered the national anthem of Black America.

Aunt Barbara stood up and walked quickly to the door. Before she stepped into the darkness, she turned back to everyone in the kitchen who had started singing along and said, "Okay, she's here." Karen had arrived. I was excited and relieved. Finally someone I could talk to.

A spotlight cut a path across the floor from the DJ table to the basement door. Karen stepped into the light. From the dark sidelines someone reached over and pulled away the black wool coat covering her shoulders and back. Her skin reflected the bright white beam like a halo. In her left hand she cradled a corsage of purple flowers laid out on a white tissue paper pillow in a clear rectangular box. She wore a diaphanous lilac dress with puffy sleeves and a pleated skirt. Her hair fell down her back in long curled ringlets. Karen walked slowly, like she was in a procession. She looked deliberately from side to side, smiling confidently at her guests. So beautiful. So poised. I wanted to be her. Or at least be close to her.

The DJ handed Karen a microphone. The Stevie Wonder song faded, the singing trailed off as the room burst into applause. Over the clapping, Karen said, "Thank you for coming. This is going to be a good party. With good food. And good people. So come on, let's have a good time." She handed back the microphone, and a crowd of guests closed around her like the shutter of a camera.

I pushed my way through and waited, facing Karen as she hugged one of her friends with her eyes shut tightly. When she opened her eyes she gave me a big smile and reached over her friend to pull me close. We rocked back and forth, in sync like a metronome. I heard someone say, "That's her cousin." Then, "Don't they look like sisters?" Karen pulled away and held my shoulders in her hands. She looked me in the eye with the intensity of someone about to share a secret. I leaned in, ready and eager to hear whatever she had to say. But she only asked me if the party was fun. Was I having a good time? "Yes," I said. "Yes. This party is the best, Karen. It's just the best." She smiled as she rubbed my shoulder, then stepped into the crowd of guests and was gone, leaving me with the faint sweet scent of lavender and vanilla on my skin and clothes.

Something soft and slightly scratchy rubbed against my arm. My father nudged my wool coat against me and said, "Here. We're leaving."

I was stunned. "But Karen just got here," I said.

"We've been sitting here for two hours. I don't have time for this nonsense. I've got things to do."

My mother rushed up, pulling her hands through her coat sleeves. She was out of breath. I realized by the scowl on her face that they had already argued about this. I knew my father's mind was made up, but that never stopped my mother from trying.

"Ricky, wait. Can't we stay just a little longer?"

"That child made all these people wait. For what? So she could make an entrance?"

I thought of all the times my father had made us wait. He'd

stop to drink coffee or smoke a cigarette or drink coffee and smoke a cigarette while everyone was already dressed and ready to go somewhere. He would sit in his silk pajamas at the small desk with the telephone in the foyer. Looking out the window, listening to Sarah Vaughan or Chris Connor with smoke swirling around his head. Only when he was good and ready would he saunter upstairs and start to get dressed.

Or he'd back out. At the last minute. He would say matter-of-factly to my mother that he wasn't going. That he'd changed his mind about attending my elementary school graduation.

He almost didn't go to my sister's high school graduation, because she refused to let him write part of her salutatorian speech. He wanted to rail against the Black students who had bullied my sister and made her feel like an outsider for being smart. And the white classmates and teachers who'd tried to make her think she wasn't smart enough to be salutatorian—an honor based strictly on grade point average. After several cups of coffee and just as many cigarettes, he decided to go. We were late. But they couldn't start the ceremony until she got there.

That suited my father just fine. He had controlled the situation and thought he'd taught them a lesson. Just like he was trying to teach Karen a lesson by punishing her with our early departure. But the only person being punished now was me. My disappointment felt like rocks in my stomach.

"She's a child, Ricky," my mother said.

"You want to stay? Go ahead."

My mother looked at me, and I could tell that she shared my disappointment.

"Maybe we will," she said and stopped following my father toward the door.

"Oh, so you know how to get back to Queens from here?" my father asked.

My mother was directionally challenged. Most of the time my father drove, and when my mother did, we had to double back. My mother was brave but not adventurous. She didn't like driving in unfamiliar places. Even though she'd grown up in the Bronx, this part of the borough was unfamiliar to her.

"No." My mother laughed. "But I'll figure it out."

I knew she would have. But I also knew this was the last thing my mother wanted to do. She was doing this only for me, but I didn't want her getting into trouble with my father on my account. I was the only one who could talk her out of it.

"S'okay," I said to my mother. "We can leave."

We headed for the door. I looked back and saw Karen surrounded by guests. The girls who had looked me up and down, then snubbed me, were smiling now. Oohing and aahing over Karen's dress. Her makeup. Her hair. They took the corsage out of the box and slipped the stretchy little silver band over her wrist. She stood in the middle of them, being admired, turned round and round. She reminded me of the ballerina in a music box—surrounded by little mirrors, sparkling from every angle, forever spinning in the same place.

CHAPTER THREE

6 Nu

April 4, 1981

It was a Saturday morning. I was lying in the top bunk of my Ethan Allen bunk bed, above the shafts of sunlight filling my room from the window, running through SAT words in my head. *Fatuous. Facetious. Flotsam. Jetsam.* "Flotsam" and "jetsam" were giving me a hard time.

The day before, during lunch in the band room, my sophomore friend Ray played an up-tempo blues riff on his guitar and shouted out vocabulary words from a book of practice exams. I shouted back definitions to the beat, between bites of a chicken salad sandwich my mother had packed for me in a green plastic lunchbox. I had figured out how to turn lunch into a "service period," working for teachers who mostly left me alone in an empty classroom to help them complete menial paperwork. So instead of gossiping in the lunchroom and ogling cute boys, who were never interested in me anyway, I organized sheet music for Mr. Serating and studied with Ray, a cherub-faced, curly-haired musical prodigy generously employing his considerable musical talents to help me boost my SAT scores.

"Fatuous" is silly. "Fat u?" Ray asked, then answered "O, us." He was being silly, so I remembered that definition, which somehow made it easier for me to remember that "facetious" meant joking, often inappropriately. "Flotsam" and "jetsam" were another story. I had never heard these words before and would have had no reason to use them. Both had something to do with parts of a ship, considered either equipment or wreckage, floating in the water. One deliberately so, the other accidentally. Subtle differences, and I couldn't remember which was which.

I propped myself up on my elbows in the top bunk. I didn't want to get out of bed. The SATs were next month. I was taking weekly practice exams in a class on Saturdays. I needed help with everything—vocabulary, math, and reading comprehension. I was a straight-A student with perfect attendance, but school never came easily to me—unlike my sister, who was salutatorian of her class of eight hundred students and on that Saturday in April was a freshman at Harvard. I had a lot to live up to and had hoped life would be easier once she was gone. But her empty room across the hall was like one of my mother's withering looks—a silent admonishment to do better.

Fatuous. Facetious. Flotsam. Jetsam.

I let those words swim around in my head, satisfied that I had a handle on at least two of the thousands of words that could be on the SAT. I threw off the covers—*Does that make them flotsam or jetsam?*—and got out of bed.

My mother was up already, buzzing around as persistently as the kitchen fan whirred. The house was full of breakfast smells, buttered toast and greasy bacon. Faint strains of the all-news radio station 1010 WINS drifted up the stairs as I made my bed. I recognized the station's musical theme—a nonsong that was the rhythmic sound of a ticker tape dispensing breaking news—followed by the tagline "1010 WINS: You give us twenty-two minutes, we'll give you the world." In less than an hour I had to pick up Lisa, my classmate and closest friend, and get to the SAT prep class on the other side of Queens.

It was my father's turn to drive us, but he was still sleeping. Across the hall, my parents' bedroom door was closed, and I didn't dare wake him.

He'd come home late the previous night. Again. My mother stayed up setting her hair and writing in her diary. Since my older sister had left for college, things had been strained between them. With my sister away, I thought there'd be more space for me in the home, not less. But my father remained elusive. There was always gardening, storm windows to be put up, things to be fixed down in the basement or out in the garage. I wasn't good at talking politics, banking, race relations, or foreign affairs like my sister. I wanted to be an actress, which distressed my father enough to warn me that there wasn't any work for actresses who looked like me. Not brown enough to be cast as Black or light enough to pass for white. People were always asking me, "What are you?" My father told me, "You'll end up a hooker on Forty-Second Street." I was used to the sting of his words, but his warning gave me pause.

My mother stood at the bottom of the stairs and yelled, "Ricky, get up! You have to take Elle to SAT class."

"You take her!" my father yelled back, then almost immediately added, "Can you take her, Mel?" Softening my mother's name to a nickname he reserved for apologies and outrageous requests. That didn't stop my mother from storming up the stairs and throwing open the bedroom door. A heated negotiation ensued. I didn't want to be the cause of another fight.

I stepped deeper into my closet and focused on finding something to wear.

The SAT class was full of cute boys from other schools and lots of pretty girls who came dressed to impress them. Lisa was as nerdy as I, with her glasses and braces, but her petite frame and curly permed brown hair made her a crowd-pleaser who drew double takes then soft smiles that rendered me invisible even when I was standing right next to her. I was desperate to be noticed by the opposite sex, but clueless as to how. I was tall—five feet ten by eighth grade—awkward, and out of proportion. I had a flat chest, broad shoulders, and arms that were too long for any shirt with sleeves to fit properly. Long legs with thick thighs meant most jeans never made it past my knees, and any pants that did manage to make it all the way up were high-waters.

I breathed in the thready smell of clean cottons and wools mixed with the dry old cedar walls surrounding my wardrobe. My closet was small, only two rows for clothes, and the back half was full of my mother's out-of-season outfits. I'd spent most of my life—kindergarten through eighth grade—neatly tucked into a gray-and-maroon plaid Lutheran parochial school uniform. All the other clothes my sister and I wore were ill-fitted hand-me-downs from my mother's friends' daughters or dressy outfits bought new for special occasions like Easter Sunday or my sister's high school graduation. I wanted my own clothes but buckled under the pressure of having to decide what I liked. I missed the simplicity of wearing the same thing every day in elementary school and the safety of not having to express myself through an outfit.

Finding clothing that fit my body was difficult.

Finding clothing to fit my personality was impossible.

At my high school you had to pledge allegiance to either the land of disco or the country of rock. I watched *Soul Train*, Deney Terrio's *Dance Fever*, and Andy Gibb on *Solid Gold*, but I also had a subscription to the Columbia Record Club, where I bought albums for a penny by Aerosmith, Jethro Tull, and Kansas. I didn't look good in the velour tops, headbands, or leg warmers favored by my disco contemporaries, or the ripped jeans, concert T-shirts, and denim jackets with band album covers painted on the back worn by the rock 'n' roll boys and girls who both sported long, feathered hair. I wore button-down shirts with handmade trousers sewn by a tailor using the leftover fabric from my father's bespoke suits and lugged around an unattractive brown leatherette bag that sagged under the weight of my textbooks. I would have been another faceless nerd in honors classes had it not been for my scene-stealing turn as a crazy ax murderess in the school play. Bug-eyed, standing on a chair and gesticulating wildly, unconcerned for once with what my classmates thought, because that's what the part required. That's what I loved about acting: a chance to be free of myself.

Everyone knew who I was, but no one knew me. Including me.

I heard the phone ringing and dressed quickly. I assumed it was Lisa's mother asking where we were. I didn't answer it. Neither did my mother, who popped her head into my room. "Okay, good, you're dressed. Now you go downstairs and grab breakfast. I'll put my shoes on and be right there. I'm driving you." As I headed downstairs 1010 WINS blared from the clock radio in my parents' bedroom. The mattress springs creaked, my father lumbered out of bed but only to hit the snooze button. The radio went silent.

"Ten more minutes," he said before crawling back under the covers.

The phone stopped ringing.

I sat in the front seat of my mother's Toyota Camry, eating pieces of crispy bacon from a balled-up paper towel. She was wearing a housedress. Her hair was wrapped in a silk scarf. She turned the radio on, rolled down her window, then lit a cigarette. Clouds of smoke rolled out of her mouth as she talked about "your father."

"If he thinks he's going to keep getting away with this shit, he has another thing coming." I half-listened as we drove away from Hollis, under the Long Island Rail Road overpass to the other side of the tracks. I looked out the window at the palatial homes of Jamaica Estates made of red brick and stone. We passed Saint John's University, where my mother had completed her master's in bilingual education, where my sister had conducted research and won a prestigious Westinghouse science scholarship, and where the previous semester I'd made out in a locked entryway with the third boy ever to ask me out on a date.

My sister had wanted to go to Saint John's, to live at home, to not leave my parents until they convinced her to accept the offer from Harvard. Now she was happy.

I was worried about taking the SAT, about getting stuck in Queens, about never leaving my parents' home.

We crossed the avenue toward Lisa's. The houses were smaller, closer together. My mother slid the scarf off her head, fluffed up her bangs. She announced what would happen next: She would wait in the car. I would get out and ring the bell but not visit. We were already late.

That's when the news came on the radio.

"Last night a sixteen-year-old girl was shot to death in a robbery at a Burger King on White Plains Road in the Bronx. The victim, Karen Marsh, was the daughter of a homicide detective with the NYPD. A search for the suspects is currently underway."

My mother gasped, we both looked at the radio, and she said, "What?" She ran a red light, slammed on the brakes too late, and skidded into the intersection. Horns blared. I pressed my palms against my chest to still my pounding heart. Mouth agape, stunned into silence, I looked at my mother.

"Oh dear God," my mother said. Her eyes darted wildly up and down the intersection. "Let me get out of here." She put both hands on the steering wheel and joined the tide of traffic. We sailed down streets, careening toward Lisa's house. "We'll tell Lisa you can't go to class, then we're going home. Okay? Okay?"

I couldn't answer.

My mother grabbed my hand and shook it. "Are you all right?"

I gulped at air like I was drowning.

"Answer me, are you okay?"

I nodded but did not speak. "Flotsam" and "jetsam" swirled into my head. Jetsam was a ship's parts deliberately put out to sea, jettisoned to lighten the load of the vessel. Flotsam was not. Flotsam was parts dislodged violently, cast into the ocean by accident or distress. All at once I understood—flotsam dislodged, distressed, floating wreckage.

My mother double-parked; I ran up the steep brick stoop to Lisa's house and rang the bell. Lisa's mother answered the door wearing a polite but thin smile. I could tell she was annoyed, until she looked at my heavy, downcast eyes and gently lifted my chin with the crook of her index finger. Her face went slack.

I stumbled, trying to explain, "My Karen, my cousin . . . she's—" I couldn't bring myself to say the word "dead." "She was shot. Killed. It's on the radio. I can't go to class today. Tell Lisa I'm sorry."

She squeezed my shoulder. "Oh, honey," she said.

I nodded, acknowledging the awfulness of the news, and then for some reason I smiled. To make her feel better, even though I was the one in pain. I had learned not to burden others with my emotions. Ashamed and embarrassed, I turned away and headed back to the car. Lisa came to the door.

"Slime?" she called, using one of the nicknames we had for each other.

I heard the confusion in her voice, the concern, but kept moving. I wanted to go home.

When my mother and I got back to our house, I ran in the back door and heard the phone ringing again. My father didn't answer it. I sped up the stairs, expecting to find him busy, putting on his shoes or shaving. But he was still in bed, eyes closed, breathing deeply, covered up to his neck in a blue wool blanket and a white cotton sheet. My mother pushed past me, put a hand on his covered shoulder, and shook him once, firmly, out of sleep.

"Ricky," my mother said. "Wake up."

My father opened one eye and barely lifted his head off the pillow. "You're back? What's the matter?"

My mother hesitated, and I was glad she had pushed past me, that I wasn't the one giving my father the news. I didn't know what to say or how to say it. I looked at my mother, curious as to how she would tell my father that Karen was dead. And not just dead, but shot. Murdered.

My mother's face twisted in pain. She said, "Karen was killed last night."

My father bolted upright in bed, then burst into tears. In an instant his face was wet as a washcloth. His hands grabbed the sheets. He dug the heels of his clenched fists into his thighs and wailed, long and low, as if he were some great wounded, four-legged beast. Then the word slipped out across his lips in a guttural moan.

"No," he said. Only once, but his voice wavered, so it sounded as if he was saying it over and over and over again: "No, no, no." As if saying the word would stop the pain or change the outcome of events.

"I thought it was a dream," he said. "I heard it on the radio but I thought I was dreaming."

My mother took a seat on the edge of the bed and turned away from my father with her chin resting in her right palm. Her left hand held my father's ankle. She closed her eyes as if she couldn't bear to see my father railing against life, or in this case, death.

I saw every detail of my father's face. The veins in his neck, the creases around his eyes. I smelled my parents' bedroom, the dry heat from the morning sun lifting dust off the worn wooden slats of the imperfectly closed venetian blinds; the slept-in cotton sheets, musty with sweat and my parents' commingling. I heard the faint buzz of the minute hand sweeping around the face of the electric clock radio and knew at any moment the alarm was set to blare out the news of Karen's murder again.

I was afraid.

I had never seen my father cry before. Not like this. I had seen him cry from laughing too hard. His shoulders would shake, racked by big air-gulping spasms. His eyes would shut tightly. His lids would soak with tears that he wiped away slowly and easily with a finger. But I had never seen him cry out in pain, either physical or emotional. This, it seemed to me, was both. The tears were so plentiful they seeped out of his closed eyes and ran down his cheeks in rivulets onto his lap. I watched the drops change the navy silk sheets to a darker, deeper shade of blue. I stepped back into the hallway, because being close might make the pain splash onto me.

Also, I wanted a better view.

I wanted to see it all and not be told to leave by my parents. But a part of me had already left. An emotional separation had occurred. My father was vulnerable, and I was stronger than I thought. I distanced myself from my father's pain and somehow knew everything was about to change.

CHAPTER FOUR

April 4, 1981

I was watching my parents from the hallway when the phone rang. The shrill bell pierced the still air, now weighed down with sorrow like a sopping-wet towel. My mother's body tensed the way it did when a neighbor or one of her girlfriends stopped by unexpectedly. My parents didn't like intrusions at home. We were forbidden to ask classmates over to visit, to do homework, or to have dinner. Company was for holidays and "occasions" deemed special by my parents. So when the phone rang, my sister or I was dispatched to run interference with several ready-made excuses. "He's outside working in the yard." "She's taking a nap."

My mother pulled herself up from sitting on the edge of the bed and answered the call. She said hello in a clipped, irritated voice. Her body softened, so I knew it was Aunt Barbara on the other side. Aunt Barbara had been calling our house all morning, trying to tell us about Karen's murder before we heard it on the radio. My father rushed downstairs to listen in on the extension. I watched my mother. She steadied herself against the tall bureau, propped up on her elbows, with the beige Princess phone pressed to her ear. She closed her eyes and shook her head slowly back and forth in disbelief and despair.

"Oh, Barbara. Oh dear God, dear God," my mother said. "What happened?"

Karen and a skeleton crew of kids had been working the graveyard shift on Friday night at the Burger King near White Plains Road. It was almost time to lock the double glass front doors when two boys entered and headed straight for the counter. One of the boys held a sawed-off shotgun. They demanded all the money from the register. Karen was standing at the till. She slid the drawer open and handed over all the cash—$241. The boy holding the sawed-off pulled the trigger. He shot Karen at point-blank range. The fiery blast blew her face off. Her body was lifeless before it even hit the ground.

Karen was killed in an instant.

The two boys scrambled out the doors and sped off with a third assailant in a car that had been idling at the curb.

My mother drew her head down to her chest. Her thumb and index finger rubbed the wrinkled creases of her forehead as if trying to coax out a rational explanation for what had happened.

"But she gave them the money. Why did they have to shoot her?" my mother asked. As if the "why" mattered. As if an answer could make this right.

I had questions of my own.

I tried to picture where Karen worked. A city block, lined with storefront businesses, most of them closed at that hour. The street empty. The air chilly, the concrete cold and hard. An el train rumbling overhead, stopping with the screech and spark of metal on metal. Doors sliding open; a garbled voice filling the open-air platform and announcing the station. Electronic bells chiming as the doors tapped closed. The train chugging away. And then an old American-made car with three hard-faced boys pulling up underneath the tracks and parking at the curb.

I tried to picture Karen inside, working. Wearing a brightly colored uniform with a matching baseball cap. Her long, curly hair trapped beneath a net. Standing behind the counter, taking care of the last customer with a smile on her face.

One maybe two people sitting in the two-toned hard plastic seats made to look like they were cushioned so you'd sit and eat, but not stay too long.

It was late, almost midnight, when the world feels shrouded in deep, plum darkness. Music from the radio playing in the background, to help pass the time, to keep the kids company as they cleaned up under the sting of fluorescent lights. Wiping down the kitchen, emptying the garbage, before the glass double doors with the silver handles pushed open and two young men strode up to the counter.

Did Karen see the robbers coming? Or did she turn to face them, with a ready smile and the words "May I take your order?" on her lips? What did they say? "Give us the money"? "Hand it over"? Did they need to say anything? When did she notice the sawed-off shotgun being lifted and pointed at her face?

I tried to picture Karen looking down the barrel of the shotgun. Was she scared? Surprised? Confused? How long did she stare into that abyss of the barrel before turning her eyes down to the register? Fumbling over the keys to open the drawer. To scoop up the cash. Two hundred and forty-one dollars. Was it fifties, twenties, or tens? A one-dollar bill or a handful of change? When she gave it to the robber, did her shaky hand touch his sweaty palm? Or did she set it all down on the counter for him to pick up?

However it happened, he took the money and started to leave. Karen stayed. She waited for him to go. Karen, the good girl, stood there. Like a target. Paralyzed by fear. Or maybe flooded with relief that it was almost over. Staying perfectly still until it was safe to move again, to breathe. I imagined that she held her breath. But I wondered if, when the shotgun went off, she gasped, took one last inhale of life. Did she know that was what she was doing?

"I'M GOING TO THE BRONX," my father announced as he rushed back into my parents' bedroom. He fished around in the drawer where he kept his monogrammed money clip and keys, the leftover coins from our vacations abroad and souvenir pendants from around the world, his cuff links and tie clips, and a box of bullets. He stepped back empty-handed, peered into the closet where he kept two of his guns—one in a shoebox on the floor, the other in an unlocked lockbox on the shelf. He didn't kneel down or reach up; he stood still—staring. After a moment, he ran his hand over the sleeves of his dark suits and the arms of his crisp white shirts. He seemed lost, trapped on the small square of rug between the dark closet and the bulky heaviness of the wood dresser.

"We'll go with you," my mother said. Her words jarred my father into action. He nodded, then pulled a pair of trousers off a hanger.

I rushed into my room and unpacked my book bag. I took out my dog-eared SAT study guide and let the fibrous pages flip over my thumb before sliding it under a stack of books on my shelf for what I was sure would be the last time. I couldn't imagine going back to SAT class now that Karen had been murdered. I was weighed down with a crushing disappointment. There was nothing left to look forward to, so why even try? Learning SAT words felt pointless.

I sat in the living room in a wingback chair across from my mother slouched behind the clunky Ethan Allen pinewood desk. We both looked off into space, transfixed by the nothingness in the middle distance—the thousand-yard stare; in World War II, that's what they called the traumatized look in the eyes of some soldiers who survived the battlefield.

I tried to picture a sawed-off shotgun, but I didn't know what one looked like. I'd seen plenty of handguns. Held them. Shot them. Even taken one apart, with my father's help, to clean it. I watched, awed, as he reassembled it with grace and ease. My father had 9-millimeters, .28-calibers, a .45, and that snub-nosed .38 with the taped-up grip. Made by Smith & Wesson, Remington, and Colt. He had revolvers and semiautomatics.

He didn't have shotguns or rifles. He wasn't a hunter. He didn't shoot things for sport.

Those types of guns were scary to me. Those were guns meant to kill, not protect, like my father's guns. A sawed-off shotgun sounded even scarier. I imagined the jagged teeth of a saw jutting out around the barrel, pointed at Karen's face.

Point-blank range.

I'd heard that term but never had to consider it before. But there it was. "Point blank" as in zero, no distance at all.

I heard my father's footsteps pound heavily into the plush carpeting upstairs. He moved in quick, purposeful bursts, then stopped for long pauses, then stomped and stopped again. The bathroom door slammed, water ran, an electric razor hummed. He came down the stairs clean shaven, smelling of bay rum cologne, wearing custom-made wool trousers with a sharp crease down the front, and a suit jacket over a starched white long-sleeve shirt with cuff links and no tie. The .38 nestled in his ankle holster.

My father looked like he was going to work.

He headed into the kitchen and made himself a cup of coffee, then sat in the front room at the telephone table. He lit a cigarette and picked up the phone.

He called the "guys from the job"—that was how my father referred to the core group of parole officers he worked with, the ones he partnered with and trusted with his life when he made home visits or tracked down absconders to make an arrest. Joe Isherwood, Calvin Moy, and Ernie Hobson, who was nicknamed "the Dove" for his accommodating personality—in contrast to my father, nicknamed "the Hawk" for doing home visits on parolees at three o'clock in the morning. According to my father, "Most law-abiding citizens are supposed to be home in bed at three a.m."

I saw the "guys from the job" only on special occasions—Moy's twentieth anniversary, Isherwood's book signing, a restaurant opening for one of Ernie's friends—but I heard stories about them, their girlfriends, and their families around my family's dinner table. I didn't know why my father felt the urgent need to consult with them now, when we were waiting to go to the Bronx to find out what had happened to Karen.

"Cal, it's Richie," my father said into the phone. "Yeah, not so good. My niece was murdered in a robbery last night . . . Yeah . . . Thank you . . . Warren's little girl . . . Yeah, yeah, Karen. Out at that Burger King on White Plains Road . . . You heard about that? Ain't that something . . . You damn right. That's why I wanted to talk to you. Who do we know out there? . . . Could you? That would be great. Yeah, yeah. Hold on a minute."

My father glanced over his shoulder at me, then lowered his voice. He repeated the phone call several more times. I couldn't hear what he was saying anymore.

My mother emerged from the fog of her thoughts. "Dear sweet Jesus," she said. "They blew her face off." It was as if the words were just starting to make sense. My mother looked at me. "There but for the grace of God."

"Yeah, right." My father, an atheist, spat out a laugh. He was standing over us now, fingers twitching impatiently against his leg as if we had been the ones keeping him waiting. "Let's go."

I slid into the back seat of my parents' dingy maroon Camry. My father always drove with the window cracked open. He flicked the smoldering ash from his cigarette out through the opening, but the wind knocked the little gray flecks back onto me. I inched over to sit behind my mother, out of range of my father's ashes. Usually I liked being in the car, looking out the window, watching the world pass by. That day I barely lifted my head. The news station rebroadcast the story about Karen's murder. My father turned off the radio. We drove in silence to Karen's house.

I remembered it as a pretty little street crammed with two-family houses made of red brick or painted clapboard with wide wooden porches. Karen lived there, in a cluster of homes owned by my aunts, uncles, and grandmother on my father's side of the family. People sat out in wicker rockers during the spring and summer months, and made leaf piles or built snowmen in the fall and winter. The front yards were full of flower gardens and protected by galvanized steel fences that doubled as playground equipment for climbing on, jumping over, and sticking tennis balls inside the diamond-shaped chain links.

I understood why some people mistook this for a bad neighborhood. It was off White Plains Road down the block from the el train and an avenue full of sketchy storefront shops and cheap clothing stores that looked like fronts for less legitimate businesses. As was often the case, good lived side by side with bad.

The only thing scary about the street to me was how steep it was. The street was a hill with the sharpest drop I'd ever seen. The grade of it took a physical toll. Pedestrians held their bodies at near 45-degree angles to avoid tumbling over. The house foundations were fortified on top of triangles of cement and brick just to be level. The descent made me lurch forward in the car; my hands would fly up involuntarily to brace against the back of the front seat. I worried that the car would pitch forward and send us vaulting end over end. Even my father steeled himself. He would clench his jaw and grip the steering wheel with both hands, then snap at my mother to either sit back or look out and tell him how much room he had left to maneuver into a parking spot. He'd work the steering wheel with the flat of his left palm, whipping it this way and that. Right arm lying across the back of the front seat to steady him. His head swiveling back and forth, to and fro among windshields, windows, and mirrors.

This street was not to be trifled with.

And yet my father always managed to take control.

When there was no street parking, my father would drive around the corner to an alley hidden behind the homes where all the detached garages were. We'd park behind Uncle

Charles's house. The broken city pavement of the alley gave way to a flat gravel driveway that crackled and popped beneath the wheels like an old country road. Uncle Charles had a garden of vegetables and fruits with plenty of flowering plants to lure in bees. In the summer the adults would sit on the back porch with glasses of lemonade and iced tea while us kids ran around catching fireflies in jelly jars. Uncle Charles poked holes in the lids with an ice pick and sent us back to Queens, where it seemed to me our fireflies didn't burn as bright and our lemonade wasn't as sweet. That is, until I got older and a visiting relative cornered me in a back bedroom.

He slid his hands underneath my shirt. He felt my fourteen-year-old breasts through my new training bra. The heel of his palm was soft and cool even as it pressed hard into my lower ribs, holding me in place. I stood still, stunned, with my back against an ornate wooden chest of drawers, my hands held up in a gesture of surrender.

"Thank you," he said, then moaned. "Oh, you make an old man feel so good. And you filled out so nicely. Why don't you let me see how nicely you've grown in?"

Before he could go any further, I pushed past him and skittered out the doorway.

I slipped into the living room, where Karen was sitting with the rest of the family, visiting with my parents. She was mid-story about the goings-on at her Catholic girls' school. Everybody laughed. Burning with shame, I sank into a corner of the couch. Disgust tickled the back of my throat. As soon as we got home that night, I told my mother what had happened. Her mouth dropped open in disbelief, then closed tightly, lips pursed together. She said, "I'll take care of it." Then she leveled her gaze at me. "But don't you go telling your father about this. He'll kill that man and I don't need your father going to prison."

I knew my mother was right. I didn't tell my father. And it never happened again.

The hood of my parents' Camry crested the hill, then took a nosedive. We inched down the street. The sidewalk on both sides was dotted with clusters of people talking, whispering, nodding guiltily at Karen's house. Some were neighbors, some were neighborhood friends, most were strangers, I could tell. Not close enough to the family to go inside, they rubbernecked the true mourners who came and went through the front door, uncharacteristically left open.

The already-narrow street was reduced to one lane by a long line of double-parked cars. Unmarked police vehicles. I could tell by the red cherry lights in the windshield and the official police business placards displayed on the dash. My father pulled up to the end of the line and parked. He put his parole office sign under the windshield, then got out without so much as a glance back. I jumped out to open my mother's door and helped her onto the sidewalk.

As usual, my father stopped at Grandmother's house first. Grandma had been mugged twice when she lived in the projects. She was attacked in the elevator, then the stairwell. Frightened but still angry the first time, she refused to move. The second mugging put her in the hospital, where she refused to die. That's when my father moved her onto the block with the rest of the family. She lived in a duplex, on the first floor of a house, in an apartment that smelled of cedar and musty lace. When my family came to visit we'd sit in the front parlor room with the bay window. I would eat candy from the glass jars sitting on every flat surface. Soft caramel chews, peppermint swirls, and tiny fruit-flavored logs. One after another until my mother said enough.

We always sat in the same seats. My parents side by side on the Queen Anne love seat, my sister in the wingback chair, and me moving slowly back and forth in the wooden rocker next to the end table with the music box of hymns from the Christian Science Reading Room.

Grandma would bring out fresh coffee with half-and-half for my father, tea with lemon for my mother. My sister and I would drink grape or apple juice and listen to the adults talk. I played the music box, winding it up again and again until someone stopped me—usually my mother, blurting out my name in a high-pitched voice of both annoyance and warning. Grandma would chuckle, brush the air with her fingertips, delicately but definitively waving away my mother's admonishments, saying, "Let the child play."

Grandma was small and seemingly delicate, like a statue carved of alabaster marble. Her skin was white, almost translucent in places, showing blue veins and chalky bone just beneath the surface. She was light enough to pass but never would have. She was proud to be the great-great-granddaughter of a Bermudian slave who'd earned his freedom by navigating a British ship safely through the treacherous coral reefs surrounding the island. Grandma inherited the slave's mettle; she came to America on her own at eighteen—but she seemed undone by Karen's murder.

My father rang the bell, then pounded on the front door until Grandma let us into the house.

"What's the matter? You hear me knocking out here."

Grandma sighed, pulled the ends of her sweater closer over her shriveled chest. She shuffled into the front parlor and eased herself into a chair far away from the bay window and the view of people on the street. She didn't offer us seats or anything to drink. I stood back with my mother. My father hovered over Grandma.

"We're going up to see Barbara and Warren now."

Grandma nodded. "Okay."

"You, too, Mother. Come on."

"Not now. Maybe later."

"Everyone is there now."

"I know, Richard. It's too many people." Grandma leaned her head back and winced. She brushed us away. "Go on without me."

"All right, then, let's leave her alone," my mother offered.

"What the fuck kind of nonsense is this? She's the child's grandmother."

"Ricky, don't," my mother said.

"People are counting on you. Get up. I said get up, Mother. I don't have time for this shit."

My grandmother was a church lady, a sergeant in the Salvation Army; she didn't tolerate foul language. That day she just closed her eyes. I saw tears seep through her lids, soak the creases of her crow's-feet.

"Don't talk to her like that," I said.

"What did you say?" My father wheeled around on me. I felt the heat of his gaze on my face and looked down at the floor.

My mother intervened. "All right, Ricky. We're all upset."

My father stomped out. The room shook, then went quiet.

"It's okay, Mother. You stay here," my mother said, then left.

I followed her, chasing after my father as he strode up the street to Karen's house. Uncle Charles, Karen's grandfather, paced on the sidewalk. His eyes scanned the block, head shook back and forth, lips moved as he mumbled to himself.

Uncle Charles was one of those exhaustingly jovial, outgoing men who always had a smile on his face and a joke on deck. Never in a bad mood, he made everyone call him "Pal"—probably because he'd been a Pullman porter and didn't want anyone to make the mistake of ever calling him "boy." "Come talk to your old Uncle Pal," he'd say and pat me reassuringly on the shoulder. Then he'd fix me with those rheumy hound-dog eyes and listen as though what my six-year-old self had to say was the most important thing in the world.

Uncle Charles had a bald head. He was the color and shape of a yellow sweet potato. His trousers were always ironed with a crease, and pulled slightly higher than his waist by suspenders over a short-sleeve button-down cotton shirt, open at the neck, revealing silver-gray hairs growing like weeds out of his chest. He liked to amble up and down the block with a brown bag of store-bought sweet treats that he'd pass out to the neighborhood kids. He'd lean against a neighbor's chain link fence, arms draped over the top, "conversating" and cracking jokes that were groaningly amusing but made funnier by his good intentions and eagerness to please. Pal was everybody's friend.

Up ahead of us I saw my father slow just long enough to pat Uncle Charles on the shoulder. Uncle Charles's eyes were cast down, head shaking, lips moving as he mumbled to himself. My father disappeared into Karen's house, leaving my mother and me behind to deal with the awful pleasantries of grief.

"Uncle Charles," my mother said. He grabbed her hand, squeezed it hard. "If I could've taken her place I would've. It should have been me. I wish it hadda been me."

I walked into the house behind my mother. The living room was full of people I didn't recognize, though startled recognition flashed across a few faces who thought for a second that I was Karen. My mother soon disappeared, swallowed up by the mourners.

Left alone, I lingered at the front of the room, where a small group of women sat listening to a dark-skinned girl curled up on the couch. I didn't catch the whole story. It sounded like she had been there when Karen was shot and sprinkled by shrapnel from the shotgun blast. I thought maybe Karen's body had fallen on top of her. The women consoled her for coming so close to death. For having witnessed Karen's murder. They rubbed her back and arms. Her lap was littered with discarded tissues, her body sank farther into the couch cushions. I wanted to be petted and protected and pitied for my pain. I was Karen's closest girl cousin in age and likeness and experience. I was jealous of the attention this other girl was getting. And ashamed for feeling jealousy. I had the uncomfortable feeling that I didn't belong, that I somehow hadn't earned the right to mourn because I hadn't suffered. My skin and muscles felt uncomfortable. An unctuous taste coated the back of my throat. I couldn't sit still.

I walked toward the back of the house. Aunt Maisie caught me in her arms. She was light-skinned, like my grandmother. She favored floral-print housedresses in paisley colors, with square pockets patched onto the front. Aunt Maisie's hair was fine and wispy white as a painted cloud, curled and bobby-pinned into rosettes. She wore black-framed glasses and had black hairs on her upper lip. Her mustache felt soft against my cheek when she kissed me hello.

Like her daughter, my aunt Barbara, Aunt Maisie was one

of the most even-keeled women I knew. Her face didn't betray any sadness. Etched into her features was the same bottomless love and concern she held for everyone she met. "Come on. Go get yourself some food." She led me to the kitchen door, ushered me inside.

The kitchen was close and warm with oven heat and food smells. Casseroles were everywhere. The table and counter were full of steamy Pyrex dishes of fried chicken, spareribs, mac and cheese, pork greens—comfort food. Aunt Barbara was making space in the fridge for what seemed like several weeks' worth of donated meals for the family. Her sister-in-law, my aunt Lorin, looked down at the floor, tracing the linoleum pattern with each step, phone at her ear, talking long-distance to the relatives in Bermuda, my father's side of the family. "We don't know about the funeral yet. The coroner has to do an autopsy on the body first . . . Oh, I'm sorry. No, that's okay, don't apologize . . . I know this is hard for everyone. Listen, I need to make some more calls . . ." Lorin pressed the phone hook down, consulted an address book on the edge of the sink, then dialed another long-distance number.

Barbara and Lorin attended to the mourning tasks at hand with an impenetrable, unnerving calm. They disappeared into the familiar pattern of hosting company. Taking care of others, that's what mothers always do. By tending to other people's mourning, they delayed their own. Each casserole dish represented an awkward exchange for Aunt Barbara. A gracious nod, a grateful smile, then listening to empty platitudes about better places, time healing wounds, and God recalling his angels. Ending with the casserole-giving guest dissolving into tears and Aunt Barbara comforting him or her.

Aunt Barbara wasn't crying. Or staring off into space. She

had the same slight smile on her lips as always as she cleared space in the fridge. She was making room. Even in motion there was a stillness to her.

I felt like I had to say something.

"Aunt Barbara—"

"You want something to eat?" She cut me off. "We have plenty. As you can see." She pointed to the spread, then chuckled. "What am I supposed to do with all this food?"

"Eat it." Lorin picked up a piece of mac and cheese with her fingers. She pointed a greasy finger at me. "Let me fix you a plate."

I didn't feel like eating. But Aunt Lorin was already spooning up servings onto a paper plate.

A white man in a blue police uniform stepped into the kitchen. He took his hat off and kissed Aunt Barbara on the cheek. He opened a door tucked into the corner and disappeared down into the basement. He pulled the door closed, but it didn't catch. I watched as the door inched open. After a moment I slid off the stool and wandered over to the breach.

I could smell the basement. Cold cinder blocks, detergent, and moldy wetness with a whiff of cigarette smoke tickled my nose. I heard voices, male voices, and strained to make out what they were saying. The words weren't clear, but the tone was dark and angry. I slipped onto the other side of the door, tiptoed onto the landing, and pulled the door closed behind me until the latch clicked.

Careful not to squeak the wooden stairs, I sat on the top step and leaned over onto my thighs to listen. I looked down through the exposed pipes and wooden beams and saw Uncle Warren and a room full of men, white and Black, some in police uniforms.

They were talking about the robbers, the boys who killed Karen. Trying to figure out who they could be, how to find them, and then what to do.

"Only one thing to do." I recognized my father's voice. "Kill them. Find them and kill them."

CHAPTER FIVE

It took me a full day to respond to Warren's email. I wrote back that I would get in touch with the New York State Board of Parole. But when I looked more closely at the information Warren had sent me, I noticed that the date to submit letters against the release of Karen's killer had already passed. I was relieved. I wasn't looking forward to delving back into those painful memories. Now I wouldn't have to contact the parole board and bare my soul to some faceless bureaucrat at the end of a phone line, who probably couldn't help me anyway. I realized what might help me was to finally tell Warren what Karen, and her murder, had meant to me. I wrote back:

> We've never spoken about Karen's murder and we were so very young when it happened. I can only imagine what losing her was like for you and your mom and dad and little Geoffrey. I can tell you that for me Karen's murder was a pivotal event in my life. I consider it a loss of innocence that shaped me as a person. I remember hearing the news like it was yesterday. And I have never, ever forgotten Karen, she's always in my thoughts.

Four days later, Warren responded.

> It's difficult to talk about this subject even after all these years. Our lives were changed forever.

He added that the parole board had extended the deadline for accepting letters about the killer's parole. My stomach tightened. Suddenly I wished I hadn't said I would contact the parole board. I didn't know why I was so uncomfortable. I suspected it was more than just fear of revisiting the past. But I wasn't willing to examine these feelings more closely to consider what my discomfort might reveal about me.

I procrastinated.

It took me a week to email the parole board asking for more information about the process and the letter I was supposed to send.

They responded immediately. Offered to speak with me on the phone. They explained that I could submit a written statement that would be shared with the parole board but not the killer, even though it would become part of his confidential file.

I did nothing.

They followed up with a phone call, and I watched my cell ring until it went to voice mail. When I finally returned the call, a man with a New York accent, heavy with the outer boroughs, answered the phone: "Victim Assistance." I was taken aback. I hadn't thought of myself as a victim of Karen's murder or in need of assistance. But both were true.

My tongue felt thick inside my mouth. My gums and cheeks went dry. I couldn't find the words to explain who I was or what had happened to Karen. I had the urge to tell the whole story from the beginning, from the script I was used to repeating. *When I was sixteen, my sixteen-year-old cousin . . .* But my throat tightened and trapped the words in my mouth. I swallowed hard and used Warren's email as my guide.

"I'm calling about case number 82A2130. Santiago Ramirez." Saying the killer's name out loud felt like I was betraying Karen.

"Yes," the man said. "What can I do for you?"

"I'm the cousin," I said.

"Of Mr. Ramirez?"

"No, no. Of the young girl he killed."

"I'm so sorry for your loss."

I barely got out "Thank you" as tears clogged the back of my throat.

"You take your time, dear." He waited.

"I'm Karen's cousin. Karen Marsh, that was her name, the girl who was killed. I . . . I'm trying to . . . I want to write a letter, but I want to know about . . ." I hesitated, unsure how to refer to the man who had killed my cousin. "Santiago" seemed too familiar. "Mr. Ramirez," too deferential. "Killer," too confrontational. I settled on what he was: "the prisoner."

"Okay. Sure. What do you want to know?"

Everything, I thought. I knew nothing about who this man was. What he was like. I wondered if he had earned time off for good behavior. Was he eligible for furlough? I knew a little about the prison system from all the cop shows I'd written. I'd even been inside death row at the state penitentiary in McAlester, Oklahoma. I knew that good behavior meant more privileges and freedom on the inside. Had Santiago Ramirez been a good prisoner? What had he been doing in prison for the last thirty-three years? I pictured an old Hispanic man, stooped over with a shock of white hair, a swarthy complexion, and time marked by the creases in his face. Though he would have been only a few years older than me.

"Well . . . what has he been doing?" I asked.

"In prison," he replied, stating the obvious as if that answered my question.

"Yes. I guess I mean, what can you tell me about him?"

"Let me see what's in his file."

I heard typing and made a mental note that the files were computerized.

"Okay, Ramirez, Santiago. Sentenced twenty-two years to life. Means he was eligible for parole after serving twenty-two years. And he cannot get out until parole lets him out." He emphasized each word as if to reassure me. "If that happens, he'll be on lifetime parole. That's supervision on the outside for the rest of his natural life. Says here he was first eligible in April 2003. But he was denied."

I nodded, feeling reassured. The parole board must have had a good reason for not letting him out.

"Do you know why?"

"Doesn't say. Just that parole was denied. Been denied every time."

That surprised me. "How many times has he come before the board?"

"Well, since 2003 he's been eligible every twenty-four months, so quite a few times now."

I didn't realize this had been going on for so long. And I was stricken by the thought that this process would continue for as long as he was alive. Or until he was set free.

"What has he been doing? I mean, is he taking classes or getting his GED? What kind of prisoner is he?"

"Let's see, he's housed in a medium-security facility. And he's completed nine programs."

"What does that mean?"

"Every inmate, when he comes in, he has his needs assessed.

Santiago Ramirez was assessed nine programs and he completed nine programs."

"I see."

"Says now he's in a specialized program, a labor-intensive industrial program that offers a job-skills certificate upon completion."

I assumed that must have been a good thing for the prisoner, though I wasn't sure how I felt about it. Or how I was supposed to feel. Should I be happy that the man who killed Karen was doing well in prison? Would I have felt better if he hadn't adjusted to life behind bars? If he was suffering? Was I supposed to root for his suffering? And was his suffering supposed to ease mine? I was confused and frustrated, overwhelmed by all the unknowns and unanswered questions swirling around in my head. I still had no sense of who this man was. Or even who he had been thirty-three years ago when he shot and killed my cousin. What I really wanted to know was if he was sorry for what he had done.

I was certain he was sorry to be incarcerated, locked up for the rest of his life. He would likely say anything to get free. I didn't know if he felt remorse. Real remorse, not just regret over the bad outcome of his poor decision. His file revealed nothing. I wanted to look this man in the eyes, to see for myself.

"Can I go to his hearing?" The words came out before I even realized what I was asking to do.

"Oh, no, miss, members of the public aren't allowed."

Being told I couldn't attend left me feeling like I didn't know how I would decide what kind of letter I wanted to write. That's when I realized what I was avoiding: a decision. My apprehension over talking to the parole board was starting to make sense. I was ashamed to admit I was conflicted, but I wasn't sure why. Perhaps I didn't want the responsibility of keeping a man locked up. Even Karen's killer. I asked, "Can you send me a copy of his file?"

"No, I'm sorry, that's confidential. But I can send you a transcript of the parole hearing."

When I hung up the phone, my ears were ringing, my skin tingled, I couldn't stand still. I walked around the house, trying to work off a nervous energy that had me more apprehensive than before. I couldn't do what Warren was asking. Not yet. I had reservations, and I wanted more information. I was afraid that I was headed down a path that would put me at odds with the rest of my family. I was surprised to realize that I was looking for a reason to let the killer go free.

CHAPTER SIX

April 4, 1981

We left the Bronx before nightfall. The car had become chilled from the day's lengthening shadows, and I felt the coolness of the back seat on my thighs through my pants. I sat up, watching the back of my father's head, waiting for him to turn or catch my eye in the rearview mirror. I wanted him to acknowledge what I had overheard. His eyes darted past mine, and he offered no admission as he changed lanes and weaved through stop-and-go traffic. He sped out of the residential neighborhood, under the el, onto the wide-open fast lane of 295 and the Throgs Neck Bridge. My mother fell asleep in the front seat. I looked out the window at the icy white city lights dotting the darkness like grounded stars.

Maybe I was mistaken.

I wondered if I had heard it right. I didn't want to believe that my father was plotting with my uncle and a basement full of off-duty NYPD officers to kill the boys who had killed Karen. How could my father justify another killing?

Doubt and denial conspired to protect me from the unspeakable. I wanted it not to be true. But I knew my father was capable of unpredictable acts, violence as punishment or in the guise of protection.

I remembered when I was five years old, my sister and I were walking with my father, each of us holding one of his hands. On the sidewalk across from the fast-food restaurants, the subway, and the mom-and-pop shops lining Hillside Avenue was a crazy white man punching the air, yelling, "Nigger! Niggers go home! I hate niggers!" at the top of his lungs.

My father dropped our hands and looked down at us with a scowl that I assumed meant I had done something wrong. "Don't move," he said.

I froze in place and watched him stride across six lanes of oncoming traffic. He stopped cars and buses with only a look and the palm of his hand. He walked over to the crazy old white man and punched him in the head. The old white man stumbled over into a trash can, then fell onto his knees, bewildered. My father hoisted him up by his elbow and dragged him over to a squad car where two police officers were sitting, doing nothing at all. My father leaned down to give the officers a tongue-lashing. They jumped out of their car, bent the old white man over the trunk, and cuffed him.

Fists clenched at his sides, my father marched to the crosswalk and waited for the signal before rejoining us on the sidewalk. "You don't ever let anyone talk about us like that, especially not in your own damn neighborhood," he said.

Then he took our hands and we continued walking. My little heart pounded, then swelled as fear turned into pride. My father did things other people wouldn't dare.

But I wasn't feeling proud in the back seat on the way home from Karen's. I had a queasy feeling and was reminded of when our house had been broken into.

That night, six years earlier, we'd come home from a family dinner to find the stereo stolen, the color TV gone. Thieves had used a ladder left out in the yard to climb through an unlocked second-story window at the back of the house. My father willingly admitted his stupidity in leaving the ladder out. He didn't stomp, didn't shout, didn't argue about it at all with my mother. Even when he discovered that the $2,000 cash she had withdrawn from the bank that morning and left in her dresser was gone. He was certain: "The insurance will cover it."

I was afraid my back-facing bedroom window would be the next target. My father took great pains to reassure me that nothing else would happen. But the damage was done. I felt violated.

Weeks later, the police recovered the stereo and the TV, but not the money. One of my father's friends on the force brought back the appliances when he was off duty.

I wanted details about where our things had been found and how. I kept asking questions until my father told me that he had stolen them, robbed our house for the insurance money. He needed it to cover the tuition at the Lutheran parochial school my sister and I attended.

My father thought I'd be relieved and stop asking questions, stop telling everyone how great the police were for finding our stuff. Instead I stopped talking. I was angry with him. Not because I knew he had done something wrong and broken the law. My father did things like that all the time, breaking rules even as he was sworn to uphold them. He betrayed the system because he was part of it and said he knew the system was stacked against people like him—the little guy, the average Joe, the Black man. And my father's way of thinking wasn't so different from that of the other law enforcement officers we knew—Black, white, Latino, or Asian. They all used their discretion on the job and off. To deal with the inequities in the system, they developed their own rules and personal codes. I wasn't angry at my father's criminal behavior. I was angry because his robbery had robbed me of my peace of mind. I was stung that he hadn't considered how what he had done might make me feel. I felt betrayed. Because of my father I had experienced a feeling I hadn't known before: violation.

When we got home from Karen's, my father blocked our driveway and idled at the curb, waiting for my mother and me to get out. I stood on the sidewalk and watched my parents through the windshield.

I could tell they were on the verge of an argument.

When my mother got out of the car she smiled at me and sang, "Okay," as if nothing had happened. She wound her arm around my waist, walked me through the front gate.

My father pulled away. I wondered where he was going that was more important than being with us. I suspected he was headed back to the Bronx, to look for Karen's killers.

My mother retreated to the basement. "To do lesson plans," she said. "I have to get ready for school on Monday." I heard her playing the piano. Practicing her favorite songs—"Que Sera, Sera," "Malagueña," "Besame Mucho"—in a halting, mournful way.

I turned on the light in my room and crawled into the boxy bottom bunk of my bed. Disturbing the cat, I buried myself underneath a wool blanket and the afghan of yellow, green, and pink flowers Grandma had crocheted just for me.

I lay on my back looking up at the slightly bowed metal bars holding the upper mattress over my head. I wondered if it would all come crashing down on me. I found comfort in the closeness of the space, held tight and cinched into the sheets by the hospital corners my father had taught me to make. I was grateful to be back in my room, safe. Alive. Surely nothing else bad could happen to my family.

Unless my father and uncle killed the boys who killed Karen.

My hands twitched into fists beneath the sheet.

Good. That's what they deserve.

I wanted whoever had killed Karen to suffer. The heat of shame crept into my cheeks. I knew vengeance was wrong. "Vengeance is mine, saith the lord," was what I had learned at my Lutheran elementary school. Only God can punish; the rest of us must learn to forgive. Except my father, who represented the law and rules even though he acted as if he were above it. I wished I could talk with my father about how I was feeling. I wanted to ask him, point-blank, "Are you going to kill those boys?" But I didn't dare. I'd asked him once if he'd killed anyone in the war, on the job, in the streets.

"That's a stupid question," he'd snapped and ended the conversation.

I hated being chastised. I tried not to make him angry. I worked hard for his approval. But my father was unpredictable. He hid his deepest desires, real reasons, true thoughts. The only thing I knew for sure about my father was that I didn't understand him.

CHAPTER SEVEN

I went into my closet and pulled out a rectangular box of shiny black plastic that had dulled over time. Inside were twelve cassette tapes of interviews I'd recorded with parole officers in 1990. After talking to Victim Assistance about Karen's murder, I wanted to listen to those tapes again. I was hoping for insight, a better sense of my father on the job, so I could extrapolate his wishes in the matter of paroling Karen's killer. I hoped that somewhere on the tapes someone had said something about my father that would make his intentions clearer to me.

I'd made these tapes when I was twenty-six years old. I worked for an independent film and television company housed in an old brownstone on the Upper East Side of Manhattan. The owner was a wealthy man—married to a socialite, living off their considerable trust funds—who could afford to make only socially relevant passion projects. I was hoping to elevate myself from development assistant with secretarial duties to paid writer by pitching ideas for projects the company could produce.

I pitched my idea for a TV show about a homicide detective whose extended family comes apart when his daughter is killed in a robbery. The murder not only breaks the homicide detective's heart, it destroys his marriage. His best friend, who is also his cousin, is a parole officer who becomes estranged from his own daughter when she starts acting out in reaction to the murder. And the murdered girl appears as a ghost guiding her tormented family through their grief.

My boss wasn't interested in the cop-show-as-family-drama approach, but the parole officer intrigued him.

"So now, I don't really—and excuse me for not knowing, maybe I should know—but, but, but I don't . . . but what is a parole officer, exactly?" my boss asked me.

"The person responsible for watching over convicted criminals once they get out of prison," I answered.

"Well, now that, that's interesting. That's something." Instead of a scripted series, I decided to make a documentary about parole officers, even though I had no idea what a parole officer actually did. My father kept a pair of shiny silver handcuffs in the box in his top dresser drawer, from which I gathered part of his job was to arrest criminals. But he never explained how he made a living. I never asked. I was afraid he wouldn't answer or, worse, would snap at me that it was none of my business.

All these years later I remembered the interview I conducted with the then chairman of the parole hearing board, Gerald Burke. An older white man who seemed more like a docile grandfather than the man who decided prisoners' fates. At one point in the interview, he said, "Just because you're sending a man to the electric chair doesn't mean you have to smile as you tighten the noose around his neck." I would soon learn that parole officers were full of mixed metaphors, malapropisms, and mispronunciations. He didn't know my father but was willing to talk to me because my father had been a parole officer. He said I was in the family and he could trust me. I'd taken a train to Albany just to interview him, and he'd spent all day with me. Nothing ever came of my parole documentary, but I did come to understand my father. The idea of hearing these voices from the past brought up strong memories.

I could picture him. He would sit in front of the TV, shining our shoes with a horsehair brush or cleaning his gun with a kerosene-soaked rag. Sometimes he stretched out on the couch, his lanky frame draped in a silk robe, slippered feet dangling over the sofa arm. On the floor beside him would be a plate of swiss cheese slices on Ritz crackers and an orange juice glass filled to the brim with an inexpensive wine from the local liquor store. He liked to watch cop shows on TV. *Kojak*, *Baretta*, and *Columbo.*

I would fold myself into the wingback chair across the room and watch quietly, riveted to the screen. I didn't care about the plot or the crimes, only the shows' titular characters: bald-headed Kojak in a three-piece suit sucking on a lollipop; disheveled detective Columbo wearing a wrinkled trench coat and half-loosened tie with the butt of a cheap cigar smoldering between his fingertips; and Baretta, the down-and-dirty undercover, sporting a short-sleeve sweatshirt with a jaunty newsboy cap on his head and a bright white cockatoo on his arm.

They were tough guys and mavericks. Pains in the asses who didn't play well with others and went against their supervisors. But they were dedicated to doing the right thing, even if it meant breaking the rules. They were men of action. They spoke when others were silent. Especially if it meant delivering a well-placed zinger or to say their crowd-pleasing catchphrase, like Kojak's "Who loves ya, baby?" Or Columbo's "Just one more thing . . ." These TV cops were the center of attention, but they were also loners. Confident yet humble. Charming yet intimidating. Straight shooters who kept secrets and told bald-faced lies. Unique, yet all the same. Predictable and full of contradictions—like my father. And like these TV cops, my father also had a signature style.

He shaved every morning and splashed half a palm full of bay rum cologne onto his face. He filed his fingernails, clipped his nose hairs, and trimmed the one eyebrow that grew long and stray. My father favored dark tailored suits and starched white shirts with french cuffs and chunky gold or silver cuff links. He'd put a silk handkerchief in the breast pocket but kept monogrammed white cotton hankies in his pants for his allergies. His ties were classic, beauties in solids or patterns of saturated reds and blues with the occasional diagonal yellow stripe. His leather shoes, black black or dark brown, were always polished to perfection. He put metal taps on the heel and toe to thwart the daily wear and tear.

He looked like a businessman, except he had the swagger and accessories of the streets. When he wasn't smoking, an orange-colored, mint-flavored toothpick danged from the corner of his lips. He had three gold teeth, most noticeably a gleaming left incisor. Black wraparound sunglasses shielded his eyes from the grit and grime in the city air—although he wore his shades inside as well as out. And, depending on his suit and shoes that day, he would wear a bulky tan or black leather ankle holster with his trusted .38 for protection. But the coup de grâce was my father's ghetto briefcase.

The ghetto briefcase was popular with Black and Latino men. I saw them on the subways and the streets of New York City. Plastic bags turned inside out—to hide the logo of whatever discount drugstore the bag had come from—and used as a kind of man purse. It was a place for my father to hold his temporary burdens—bills, bank statements, and whatever papers were necessary for the day's errands—plus a good book. Usually a hardback, mystery or thriller. Something by le Carré. Sometimes sociology about the state of the Black man, but always wrapped in brown butcher-block paper like my elementary school textbooks. My father didn't want people on the train to know what he was reading. He said, "That's nobody's business." He was an intimidating son of a bitch. A six-foot-three Black man with a gun and a badge and a bad attitude.

My father was the archetypal TV cop.

Except he wasn't a cop. He was a parole officer.

I visited my father's office only once when I was a little girl, on the Friday after Thanksgiving. My father never took holidays off. He knew the office would be empty and the workload light. He could leave after half a day, no questions asked. He would go in on Christmas Eve and New Year's Day, Good Friday, Easter, even the Fourth of July—especially the Fourth of July, because "this country never did anything for Black people anyway."

The Manhattan parole office was a grimy ten-story building on 42nd Street, next to the Port Authority Bus Terminal. My father held my hand as we walked into the dingy white-walled waiting room. It was empty. Fluorescent lights buzzed overhead. We passed by rows of cracked plastic bucket seats, bolted to the floor and flanked by dirty metal ashtrays, and checked in at the reception desk behind a bulletproof glass window with a handwritten sign that read ABSOLUTELY NO TALKING. Behind the glass sat a middle-aged Black woman with a full mask of makeup on her face and red talon-like fingernails wrapped around a large Greek deli coffee cup—blue and white, with a Greek-key design at the top and bottom, and the words WE ARE HAPPY TO SERVE YOU printed in the middle.

She smiled when she saw us and pressed the intercom to say, "Good morning, Officer Johnson. This your little girl? How you doing, sweetheart?"

I smiled as she buzzed us in.

We walked through the deserted bullpen. It was as vast as a city block with a skyline of vertical filing cabinets and chunky horizontal metal desks with steel rings welded to the side in case someone needed to be handcuffed.

My father had a corner office with a wall of windows that looked down on the backs of old buildings. A large metal desk the size of a small tank faced the door and barricaded my father into a corner. He didn't want his parolees to know anything about him, so he concealed his vulnerability: his family. He never wore a wedding ring. There were no pictures of my sister or me, and none of our childish drawings or the sparkly paper plate or pipe cleaner school art projects made for Father's Day. Instead he had thumbtacked up posters that said more about him than any family photo ever could: Huey P. Newton in a black leather jacket, holding a rifle and a spear, sitting in a peacock wicker chair that framed the black beret on his head like a halo; a thoughtful, bespectacled Malcolm X against a black background; Richard Roundtree as Shaft wielding a firing machine gun; and a white man's hand with a sexy Black lady as the middle finger advertising *Putney Swope*, a film by Robert Downey Sr. about a subversive Black advertising executive. Then there was the poster of Che with his scraggly beard, face in profile next to the quote "At the risk of seeming ridiculous, let me say that the true revolutionary is guided by great feelings of love."

Looking back, I wondered what the other parole officers thought about my father's choice of decor. His sympathy with

Communists and revolutionaries was surely something his white counterparts might not have appreciated or understood. But they didn't have to navigate the inherent racism of America and a justice system that, for instance, enforced Jim Crow laws and turned a blind eye to the widespread horror of lynchings. What was more curious was that racism hadn't dampened my father's desire to be a LEO (law enforcement officer) and part of that system. If anything, his sense of powerlessness contributed to his need to be in control, to subvert from the inside, to "stick it to the Man," as the saying went, by becoming the Man.

I sat quietly in one of the two metal guest chairs, my legs dangling off the puffy green leather seat cushion, and watched snowflakes tumble out of the steel-gray sky. My father drank coffee with half-and-half while he sifted through mountains of paperwork on his desk. We ate the swiss cheese on rye sandwiches my mother had packed for us in a brown paper lunch bag. He smoked a cigarette. I drank milk from a coffee mug. Parole officers wandered by to say hello. They called my father Richard, Richie, Officer Johnson, or Dick, depending on their relationship with him. They leaned against the doorway and smiled conspiratorially, pleased with themselves for getting paid to do nothing.

"Come meet my daughter," my father said, waving them closer. I shook hands with these men whom I had never heard of before, but who seemed to know all about me. They asked if I was still skiing. Playing the flute? Did I like that pogo stick my father had brought home for me?

By one o'clock my father and I were walking south on 7th Avenue to the Macy's in Herald Square to buy Christmas presents for my mother. He picked up a gift set of Shalimar perfume, her favorite fragrance, that included a round of dusting powder and a small bottle of hand lotion arranged in a deep purple box lined with dark purple silk. I selected a collection of fancy soaps because they were wrapped in paper with colorful vignettes of a Spanish señorita sitting on a balcony, walking in the street, and holding a red fan with a tortoiseshell mantilla in her hair. My mother taught Spanish at a public school in an affluent district on the outskirts of Queens. Unlike my father, she talked about her job constantly.

My mother loved teaching Spanish. Everyone wanted to be in her classes. Students in the other Spanish classes clamored to be in her annual dance program. She choreographed it to feature traditional dances from all the Spanish-speaking countries and the South Bronx. She grew up listening to Tito Puente and Celia Cruz, wearing pencil skirts with three-inch heels, and her lips stained fire-engine red. She would spend months teaching her students the merengue, rumba, and cha-cha. "That beat," she'd say, taking quick staccato stabs at the air with her hands. "Feel that beat. I love that beat." Elbows tight at her sides, she would tease out a rhythm with her hips, falling back on her heels, biting her lower lip to contain her excitement for every move. The school performance always ended with my mother being pulled onstage to a standing ovation. At Christmas and then again at the end of every school year, she was rewarded with extravagant gifts: 24-karat gold necklaces, real pearl earrings, silk scarves, leather handbags, and designer department-store chocolates that she was supposed to politely decline but never did.

My father was jealous. Teachers were beloved and admired. Parole officers were vilified and mocked. It seemed to make my father angry that my mother loved what she did and was thriving. I guessed it was because the opposite was true for him. Though I couldn't be sure; I could judge only by the few stories my mother shared about my father's job.

My mother said my father had embarrassed the department when he told a judge in open court that he wouldn't recommend paroling a female inmate who had killed three of her own babies unless she was sterilized before she was released from prison. He angered his supervisors when he violated a parolee's privacy by notifying the man's wife that her recently released husband had contracted AIDS while doing time. He annoyed his coworkers when he refused to donate at the office to various charities, yet he kept grocery bags with milk, bread, and peanut butter in the break room fridge to give to parolees in need. He defied the system by befriending a parolee after he was sentenced to life in prison for killing a police officer because my father was convinced the parolee had been framed by crooked cops needing a patsy.

My father was a thorn in the side of his bosses, but he wasn't any easier on his parolees, either. He marveled at their stupidity and frequently quoted their favored go-to excuse: "It seemed like a good idea at the time." Then he'd laugh and shake his head. He didn't trust them, so he didn't leave any aspect of their supervision to chance. He was a master of controlling people. And that control extended to my sister and me.

When my sister got her license and wanted to drive us to the movies, my father told her she could borrow the car if we took a loaded gun along for protection. My sister never borrowed the car, and I waited until I was out of the house and in college before I learned how to drive.

When I was twenty-six, in order to make the documentary,

I needed to understand my father's job. Because it would help my career, my father was willing to talk. To a point. We sat in the kitchenette, stirring half-and-half into our coffees. He lit a cigarette. I opened a window. He said, "Being a parole officer is the worst job in the world."

"Then why did you do it?"

He shifted uncomfortably in his chair. When my father was young, his nickname had been Siggy, short for Sigmund Freud. While my father liked to analyze people, he didn't want to be analyzed. Or asked questions about himself. I waited.

"Why do you want to know?"

"Because it's interesting."

"To you," my father shot back.

"Yes, to me. And presumably to you, too. You're the one who did it for thirty years."

"I didn't have a choice," he said, playing the martyr. He liked to make it seem that he had no control, when the truth was he controlled everything and everyone. It was maddening. I'd endured his rule when I was a teenager; now that I was an adult, I didn't have the patience for my father downplaying his influence. I wasn't going to let him rewrite history. I pressed, "Well, then, what did you want to do?"

"Eh," he said, taking a puff. "Have you girls and raise a family."

My mother once told me that my father had considered opening a liquor store. He had found a location and secured a loan, but for reasons known only to him, he decided against it. I couldn't imagine my father standing behind a counter, ringing up sales in a register, making small talk and change for customers. My father was not a man of modest ambition.

Though he never did share what his dreams were with me, his actions belied a great need. A strong desire to determine his own destiny and to live as he pleased.

His best friend, Alpha, was the vice president of a small savings and loan, and he would give my father tips about what stocks to buy and when to sell. My father had his eye on a plot of land for sale in upstate New York. He saved up, then borrowed $13,000 from his father-in-law. The rest of the money he got from the US government. He'd found out that the land was on a migratory path for birds, and if he let the government dig up some trees and put in a pond on the property, it would cover the difference. We spent a summer driving back and forth to the Land, as we called it. My sister and I played in the babbling brook we named Haiku Stream and watched bulldozers dig up the dirt. My father built a stone wall around the property and a rustic entrance gate made of wire, twine, and branches from felled pine trees. When the pond was finished, we floated around in lazy circles on inner tubes and caught tadpoles in plastic ice cream containers from the Gouz grocery store. My father sold the pine trees to a local lumber company and handily made back his investment and then some. The type of career my father would have been good at—finance, investing, real estate—wasn't open to a Black man in the fifties when he was looking for work. I think he felt cheated. I felt cheated for him.

"But why parole?" I asked him. "You must have had a reason."

"Because." He took a long pull on his cigarette and blew out a steady stream of smoke. "It paid good back then."

I knew he was lying. Simplifying his reason because he didn't want to say whatever the truth was out loud.

"I set my own hours. If I started early I could be done by afternoon. Then I'd go swim at the pool uptown." He smiled, remembering the cool blue water. "That was great. It was right there, up on the East Side, off the FDR. An Olympic-size swimming pool and nobody used it. Boy, that was really something."

"So you became a parole officer because you wanted to swim?" I teased.

"Yeah, yeah." He laughed.

"What did you like about being a parole officer?"

"Nothing," he said.

"You liked the people."

"Oh no. They were horrible. A lot of funny-time people on parole."

"Not the parolees. The people you worked with. You liked them."

"Not all of them."

"Calvin Moy and Joe Isherwood? Ernie?"

"Most of the guys on the job weren't like that."

"So what about the parolees?"

"What about them?"

"Did you want to help them?"

"Help them?" My father laughed. "I knew five minutes after I started it wasn't going to be what I thought."

"Really? Why not?"

"Because." He paused, then answered sincerely. "You can't rehabilitate someone who was never habilitated to begin with." Then he stamped out his cigarette and said, "Okay." I knew he wouldn't answer any more questions.

I wondered if he felt bad writing off the mostly Black and brown parolees as people who didn't know how to fit into "normal" society. This was the double-edged sword, the trickiness of being a Black LEO. Impartial judgment was tainted by what you knew to be the complicated legacy of racism in America. You didn't want to betray your people, but every day you saw how some of your people would betray you, betray the race. Black neighborhoods should be policed, deserve to be policed, want to be policed—but policed fairly. Black LEOs operated in a system in which victims who were Black were ignored, overlooked, or assumed to be criminals, and criminals who were Black became victims of the police and a criminal justice system that held them in low regard.

Being from a family of Black LEOs, I had a nuanced perspective. I wasn't afraid of the police or suspicious of law enforcement officers. They were just human beings doing a job, flesh and blood, not infallible symbols of justice. But I also didn't put LEOs above reproach just because they were "on the job." And I knew it could be tricky for Black officers—they were questioned as either traitors to the race or not to be trusted on the force. Black LEOs had to be tough, have the courage of their convictions, and think for themselves—like my father. Impressionable minds wouldn't last.

A week later my father told me he had talked to a couple of guys on the job. "I'll give you their numbers. They're expecting your call." Ernie was at the top of the list.

Ernie Hobson had been my father's partner throughout the years. He was a decade older, stout, dark-skinned with kind eyes and a gravelly voice that tumbled easily into laughter. He said parole officer was the only job he could find that "would let a Black man carry a gun and a badge and not wear a uniform." Like my father, Ernie dressed up to go to work. He wore a black fedora with a little feather sewn into the ribbon.

He told me about house parties in the early days, where you'd see all these nice cars parked out front—Cadillacs and Buicks, Lincolns. "Guys would be standing around, wearing dark sunglasses and sharp suits. All the neighbors walking by would want to know, 'Whose party is that?'" Ernie puffed out his chest. "Parole officers, that's who."

Ernie lived in Harlem, in the same neighborhood as many of his parolees. When he first started, the department assigned him only Black parolees because he blended in and would be able to check up on people without drawing attention to himself. Ernie took offense. "I wasn't having any of that. I didn't want just Black parolees, my people. So I told my supervisors. And the boss man said, 'Well, we'll fix him.' Don't you know they gave me a caseload all the way downtown. Little Italy. All mobsters, every single one." Ernie was so tickled he laughed until he coughed. "Their eyes would go wide when they saw a *moulinyan* standing at the door. That's what they called us, 'moolies.'" Ernie shrugged; he didn't seem bothered. "But then they'd invite me in for a little cannoli and cuppicino." He mispronounced the word. "I never had a problem with the I-talians," he said. "We got along great."

Because I was Richie's daughter, Ernie invited me to his home, where we could sit and talk face-to-face. He was a confirmed bachelor, living in a two-story condo with a concrete balcony overlooking the river. He had shag carpeting, shiny metallic wallpaper, and more than one black velvet painting of a naked Black lady kneeling or reclining like Ingres's odalisque on an animal-skin rug. Ernie sat in a chair next to a slow-moving purple lava lamp that had seen better days.

"You have to understand, as a parole officer I wear two hats. I'm a social worker and a police officer. My job is to try to help you get back on the straight and narrow. But if you don't or you can't or you won't—you see—well, then, my job is to arrest you. I'ma snatch your behind off the streets and send you back to Sing Sing fast fast."

"How do you know if they've done something wrong?" I asked.

"I've got a list of conditions. Things you supposed to be doing. Or not supposed to be doing. Like drinking, taking drugs, fraternizing with a known criminal element."

In other words, controlling people's behavior. Even down to who they could be friends with.

"More like who they can't be friends with," Ernie explained. "If I say you can't be socializing with this one and that, or so-and-so over there, then you can't. Period. I can Breathalyzer you, drug-test you, blood-test you. Poke you, prod you. I can do whatever I want to you, make sure you living the way you supposed to."

"But how do you know?"

"'Cause I'm watching you. Twenty-four/seven, three sixty-five. I'm going to visit you at your home. Then I'm going to show up at your job, make sure you're working. Then you're going to come see me at my office once a week. Show me your bills, your pay stubs, your receipts. You have to account for all the time when you're not standing right in front of me. You see, parole is prison without walls. And every parole officer is a warden."

My father may have been a warden, but that meant he was in prison, too. I wondered how much of my father's personality had been shaped by being a parole officer, or if he was suited to parole because of who he already was. I told Ernie my father didn't believe parolees could be rehabilitated. He nodded like he understood, but then he said, "Thing you have to understand is these are people who have been failed by every institution society has to offer. Schools don't teach them nothing, churches can't help, communities don't want them. They were dragged up, not raised."

"But you seem to believe," I said.

"Well, now, you got to listen to me here. The system is broken, that's a fact. Our resources were cut. Prisons became just warehouses for human life. Didn't teach people anything. Because taxpayers didn't want to pay to better a criminal. But what they failed to realize was if you don't pay now, you gonna pay later. Either you get these people out, on the street and acclimated, while someone's still watching them and they under your supervision, or society is gonna pay when they max out and are let out of the prisons on their own, with no one to look after them, tell them right from wrong. And that's when you start paying with the blood of your family and friends and neighbors, when your loved ones are raped and beaten or murdered by one of these guys who didn't learn their lesson, who society has failed."

I thought about the price Aunt Barbara had paid when Karen was killed. Her marriage to Uncle Warren fell apart. My cousin Warren withdrew and never seemed quite the same to me. Her youngest, baby Geoffrey, was only two when Karen was shot and grew up never knowing his big sister. For weeks after the murder he sat by the front door, wide-eyed and waiting for her to come home. He pointed to her bedroom and called out "Karen? Karen?" over and over until Aunt Barbara couldn't take it anymore. She took little Geoffrey to the cemetery, put his finger on the letters of Karen's name cut into the granite tombstone, until he understood. "This is where Karen lives now."

IT WASN'T UNTIL AFTER I talked to Ernie that I finally understood what my father did "on the job." I realized I had been raised like I was a parolee.

I listened to all twelve tapes but didn't hear anything about my father taking a stand on parole for Karen's killers. I remembered the last time I had asked my father about Karen's killers. I was writing another ripped-from-the-headlines episode for TV about drug dealers in Washington Heights who killed two undercover cops. I was looking for real-life plot twists and somehow ended up asking him, "How did you and Uncle Warren figure out who killed Karen?"

"We shut down the drug dealers."

"Drug dealers? Really? Why?"

"Because. They know everything that happens in the streets."

"How'd you shut them down?"

"Told them they weren't going to make any money until they found out who killed Karen and told us where to find them."

"And then what?"

"Then we'd take care of it."

"How?" I asked. My father knew what I was asking and shifted in his seat, annoyed at the question. A question I knew the answer to, but needed to hear him say out loud. Decades later I was finally able to admit to him that I knew what he was up to that night. I wanted him to explain, to own up to his intentions, and maybe even take responsibility. I told him,

"I overheard you. At Aunt Barbara's house, the day after Karen was killed. You were in the basement with Uncle Warren and all those cops. You were talking about killing the boys who had killed Karen." I believed he would have.

He looked at me, no remorse, no regret, no trace of a smile on his lips. "Seemed like a good idea at the time."

CHAPTER EIGHT

April 5, 1981

I woke in the middle of the night. Early Sunday morning. Still wearing my clothes. The light was on. The house was still. Across the hall, my parents' bedroom door was closed. My father must have come back from the Bronx.

I wished it were summer already, when the days lasted longer and I could sleep with the windows open while the calming whir of the fan eased thoughts out of my head and coaxed in hazy dreams. When, except for the small warm round spot where the cat had been, the cotton pillowcase and sheets stayed cool against my skin.

Bothered by the buzz of the fluorescent bulb overhead, I leapt out from under the covers to flip off the light. Racing the darkness, I dove back into the safety of my bottom bunk. I quickly pulled up the musty sheets and blankets to cover my chin, put a pillow protectively over my neck, my face.

My body was exhausted, my mind spent. Before long I was swallowed by the mattress and dropped into the deep well of sleep.

Sometime later I floated up and off the bed. As if the weight of my body could have been buoyed by the stuff of dreams and molecules of heat. I drifted into the middle of my room.

Suspended above the navy blue carpet, I was paralyzed but not panicked, because I was not alone. I felt an essence. A spirit. Karen.

She warmed my body like a golden molten light, slowly seeping into my spongy skin and porous bones. The sweet shock of her soul passed through me like a sigh, taking my breath away. Light-headed and elated, I wished Karen back. But she was gone. And I was in my bed once again. I opened my eyes and white halos dotted my vision, then dissipated into a ghostly green shimmer. I felt certain Karen had transcended the ugliness of her death. She was free. And now I was touched by her grace. Protected.

GROWING UP, I WAS afraid of ghosts. I was afraid of the dark. "Nyctophobia" was the SAT word for it. I couldn't walk into an unlit room or hallway without being overwhelmed by a crippling unease that would hold me frozen on the threshold of the dark unknown. I tried to talk myself into walking through the blackness, without rushing to turn on a light, but fear always won. By sixteen I should have grown out of it. Looking back, I realized I had been raised in fear.

It started with the bogeyman of my Lutheran elementary school upbringing: the devil. He was a red-skinned, black-horned, pointy-tailed creature with human facial features distorted just enough to be unsettling. The school chaplain at Redeemer Lutheran, Pastor Lindemann, had participated in exorcisms and spoke of them in terms vague enough to allow my childish imagination to fill in the blanks. My father assured me demonic possessions weren't real. My mother stayed silent on the topic.

I knew there were real live devils walking among us. Their exploits were front-page news. I lived through the terror that was Son of Sam and the unsettling anxiety caused by the disappearance of Etan Patz. The seventies and eighties in New York were rampant with violent crime. Hollywood made movies about how dangerous New York City was. Muggings, murder, and mayhem ruled. Stepping into a dark, confined space with a stranger was to risk your life. Alleys, stairwells, and elevators were death traps. I remember when subway cars on the E and F lines became the hunting ground for a deranged ax murderer who hacked through passengers' skulls when the train doors closed.

My parents wouldn't allow me to ride the subway by myself. Every Thursday night of my freshman and sophomore years of high school, my father would meet me in the 42nd Street subway station to escort me to an acting class at a place called the Door—A Center of Alternatives. The Door provided services for troubled youth—everything from free meals to art classes, legal aid to subsidized abortions. It was on 18th Street, in one of the old B. Altman department store buildings that took up practically an entire city block.

We would get off the F train at the 23rd Street station and head down 6th Avenue to the entrance of the Door. My father's long-legged stride forced me to walk faster. He pulled me along, holding my hand, his massive fingers wrapped around mine with a firm grip that was both comforting and crushing.

My father loved Manhattan, even with its unpredictable violence. He was a fifth-generation New Yorker. He knew the hidden history of the buildings and the city's secret stories. He shared them with me as we walked down the wide Avenue of the Americas. And even though the sidewalks were hard and unyielding, they sparkled at night, reflecting light from store window displays. It was enchanting—even after my father explained it was just glistening mica mixed into the cement to help wash the sidewalks clean when it rained.

With my father by my side, I wasn't expected to think about where we were going; he led the way.

Once we got to the Door, my father would wait two hours for me on one of the couches by the entrance. He kept his sunglasses on and sat with his legs crossed to reveal the gun in his ankle holster. He would open a book on his lap, sometimes reading, but mostly surveilling everybody with a critical eye. Meanwhile I was tucked away in the big black box theater, improvising dramatic scenes, free to act like somebody else for a couple of hours.

My mother and father had worked out a plan for how I would safely get downtown on the subway. My mother would give me one subway token from my father's stash inside his dresser drawer. I needed only one because my father would meet me on the subway, take me to class, wait for me, then take me home when class was over. My mother would drive me to Hillside Avenue, double-park at the curb with the hazards blinking, watch me descend into the subway station, then wait just in case there was a problem and she had to drive me home.

A slight panic always set in as I rushed down the dimly lit stairs to the desolate walkway, lined with grimy white tiled walls on one side and, on the other, steel bars fencing in a maze of dank stairways leading down to the platform.

My father instructed me to wait for the train by the newsstand, near the front of the station, so that I could ride in the first car with the subway driver. I was to sit facing out, so that I could see the rest of the car and not be surprised by anyone approaching from behind. My back to a wall, not a window, never next to the door, where someone could slash my face or grab my bag. If anyone tried anything, my father said, "Fight back. Make as much noise as possible. Kick, scream, they won't be expecting that. Then they'll leave you alone."

My father was always standing right where the train doors opened. When the train stopped and he saw me, the brooding scowl on his face relaxed into a broad, toothy smile. He'd kiss me on the cheek and say, "Here, here," guiding me toward a pair of empty seats. He would squeeze my hand, relieved that I had made it in one piece, then launch into a story about his day, something small and inconsequential. Maybe the post office was coming out with a good stamp or he'd finally found those two-dollar bills and brought one home for my mother, my sister, and me. Maybe he had run into a former neighbor from the block; he'd say to me, "You were too young to remember Mr. So-and-So." He delighted in the boring, non–life threatening details of everyday life. The small miracle of things not going wrong.

Then one night I got lost.

We were late getting to the subway. I sprang out of the car. Long legs straining, hair trailing behind me in a frizzy mass of curls, I raced down to the subway platform. Without looking to see which train it was, I sprinted to the front of the platform, waving at the conductor to hold the doors open. The PA warned to "watch the closing doors." An electronic bell *bing-bong*ed, the doors closed, the train pulled out. I was on my way.

But that night I missed the 42nd Street station. In my memory the train didn't stop, it whizzed by on a middle track too fast and too far away from the platform for me to even catch a glimpse of my father. I might have gotten on the wrong train or been busy doing homework and not paid attention. When the doors opened at the next station I found a pay phone and called my mother, collect. The sound of her voice nearly brought me to tears.

"Mommy," I blurted out, "I don't know where I am."

My mother didn't know the subways any better than I did. I could hear the panic shortening her breath.

"Okay. Your father called me to find out where you were. He wants you to take a train back to 42nd Street, okay? And call me as soon as you find him."

I hung up and was overwhelmed by the unfamiliar surroundings. There was a boarded-up newsstand, maps and complicated schedules enclosed in a glass display, dirty wooden benches, and people standing every which way. I was confused by the signs for Downtown-, Uptown-, Brooklyn-, and Bronx-bound trains. I rushed up and down stairs, across walkways, through pedestrian tunnels, until I finally spotted a Queens-bound train. I sprinted toward the front car and jumped in just as the doors closed. I held my breath as we approached the 42nd Street station, and exhaled as the train slowed, the metal wheels grinding against the rails and screeching to a stop. I peered out the grimy subway car window, but I didn't see my father.

The doors opened. Passengers streamed out past me, filled up the empty station, then receded like the tide into the distant exits. I stepped one foot out onto the platform for a better look and put a hand on the door to stop it from closing. My stomach churned.

My father was nowhere in sight.

I was afraid to get off the train, in the wrong place again. I was afraid to stay on the train and disobey my father's instructions. He had to be somewhere in the station. I heard "Watch the closing doors" and the electronic bell. I hopped out onto the platform. I hoped I'd made the right decision as the train doors closed behind me. Then I saw a sign announcing my location—Port Authority. The infamous bus terminal. Teeming with pimps, prostitutes, and pedophiles. Overrun by crime. Next door to my father's office, the meeting place for thousands of parolees. I realized I was on 42nd Street, but at 8th Avenue, a world away from the 6th Avenue stop where my father was waiting for me.

Panicked, I found a pay phone and called my mother collect again. She was flustered.

"Okay, your father's angry, but don't you worry about that. You just do what he says. Okay? Everything's going to be all right." She was trying to convince herself as she spoke. "He wants you to stay where you are. So don't move. Do you hear me? When he calls me back, I'll tell him where to find you."

I described where I was standing.

Fifteen minutes later I saw my father coming down the stairs. He wasn't wearing a suit. He was dressed like an undercover officer in a light blue windbreaker, sunglasses, a black plastic bag clutched under his arm. I almost didn't recognize him, but I knew the walk. That menacing swagger. Proud and threatening all at once. Part square-shouldered soldier, part boxer stepping to an opponent in the ring. My father had been both. I shrank as he came closer.

"Daddy," I started.

He shifted the plastic bag from his right hand to his left

and slapped me hard and fast across my face. Our skin smack sounded like the tip of a whip catching air. My hand flew to my cheek. My face stung with shame and salty tears.

A train pulled into the station. The doors opened. My father said, "Come on. We're going home." He grabbed my elbow and pulled me on board. I crumpled onto the hard plastic seat.

"Didn't I tell you where to stand?"

I nodded.

"Do you know where we're supposed to meet?"

I thought I said yes, but the word didn't make a sound.

"Speak up when I ask you a question," he shouted. The passengers around us looked away, quickly busying themselves with other things. I couldn't bear to meet my father's angry gaze. I closed my eyes, lifted my chin, and said loud enough for everyone to hear, "Yes, Daddy."

"Stupid," he said and shook his head—disgusted, disappointed, definitely angry. We didn't speak the rest of the way home. My father stared straight ahead. I was afraid of what he might do. To me. To my mother if she tried to defend me for making a mistake, if they got into a fight.

My mother made excuses for what my father had done. "It only happened six times," she always said. I remembered only three. Though not completely. Flashes would come back to me in snippets like the images of vampires and ghosts, or scenes from horror movies I'd watched through the fingers on my hand covering my face. It always happened at night. My father sprawled out on the couch, in the clothes he wore to do work around the house, soft heather-gray sweatpants with a drawstring and an old white cotton shirt that showed his boxer biceps. My mother at the desk, in a housedress and slippers. Lips pursed, angry. The second time she was pacing in and out, from the kitchen to the living room. "And another thing," she started, then recited her recent grievances. He looked straight ahead at the TV or he sat in the chair in the dining room, quietly reading. Silent. Still. Suddenly he would stand up and move toward her. Arm raised, then swinging down. Brutal and relentless. She was hunched, shielding her face and body with her hands, fending off blows. Scratching back when she could.

"Ricky, no. Stop it. Stop."

Once he pushed her down, onto the stair landing. Once he caught her in the dining room, behind the slatted swinging cowboy doors. The worst was when he pummeled her in the bathroom. Her body crammed into the small tub upstairs, brown ankles kicking over the side, black hair clinging to white tiles like creeping vine. He was in pajamas, she was naked under a robe that came undone, indelicately. She said it was with an open hand, always with an open hand. But I know I saw a fist and the darkness in his eyes.

"No, no." She'd break away. "Uh-uh. No. You're not doing this to me."

The first time my sister and I were little. She called us into the room.

"I want them to see what's happening. See what your father is doing?" My sister and I stood next to each other, leaning on our hands, backs against the wall.

"Call the police," she said to my older sister. "Dial 911."

My father looked at my mother, shocked and hurt.

"That's right, you heard me," she said to him.

Next thing I knew there were red and blue lights flashing, whirling around the living room walls. A white police officer took off his hat, tucked it under his arm as he talked to my mother. "You don't want to do this, ma'am."

"He hit me."

"So you say."

"I'm not going to let him hit me."

"I understand. But you don't want to do this. He's a parole officer?"

"Yes."

"He'll lose his job. You want him to lose his job? To be out of work? 'Cause that's what's gonna happen. That's no good. That's not gonna make things better. Come on. You got two little girls, a beautiful family."

My mother's face crumpled. Tears rolled out of her eyes.

"Okay. It's okay," the officer said. "I'm gonna do you a favor. I'm not going to file a report. You two work it out. You think you can do that?"

My mother glared at the officer. Through tight lips, she said, "Fine."

My father walked the officer out of the house, stood with him by the front gate. They talked, then laughed, and stole glances back at the house until the police officer put on his hat. My father shook his hand and strode back inside. He stopped in front of my mother, who stood braced, arms folded across her chest. "You made my child call the police on me," he said.

"You better not hit me again." She stared him down until he walked away.

My mother didn't keep these incidents with my father to herself. Over the years she told her sister and her friends, then balked when they responded with pity and said she should take us girls and leave.

She didn't want to leave, she wanted him to stop.

Once my sister and I were teens she told Grandma, my father's mother, whose advice was that the three of us could surely take my father down. It never occurred to me to fight back. My father was in control. And I was too afraid. But now that Karen had been killed, I wondered what the point was of being a good girl.

CHAPTER NINE

I don't remember going to church that Sunday after Karen was killed, even though I'm sure I did. I'm sure I sat next to my mother in a pew toward the back. I'm sure during the call to prayer my mother asked the congregation to pray for Karen and Karen's family. I'm sure on the way out the reverend clasped my mother's hand in his and said, "Sister Johnson, if there's anything the church can do."

In my box of keepsakes I found a gold sheriff's badge from the Christian sleepaway camp I went to when I was ten. The name of the camp, Word of Life, was etched into the metal along with a tiny blue Bible painted into the top star point. That was my upbringing in a nutshell—the law and religion. Rules. Control. I was raised to have respect for authority and blind faith in God. Even though my mother was Presbyterian and my father a devout atheist, from kindergarten to eighth grade I went to the Chapel of the Redeemer Lutheran elementary school in Flushing, Queens. Every Monday I was asked if I had gone to church on Sunday. I always had. We had chapel every Wednesday before class. And on Fridays we sang Christian songs accompanied by the hippie-dippy fifth-grade teacher, Mr. Baldinger, on an acoustic guitar. Every school day we had an hour of Bible study and were assigned verses to memorize for homework and recite out loud the next day. We said grace before every lunch. And every school day ended with a prayer and the Pledge of Allegiance to the American and Christian flags.

My father made fun of religion. He said church was for the fat, the old, and the ugly. His go-to joke was about the archangel Gabriel finally meeting God at the pearly gates of heaven and reporting back that "she's Black." His favorite poem was about a man named Abou Ben Adhem who didn't love the Lord but instead loved his fellow man. I would learn that my father's dislike of the church might have been fueled by his own anger at God and his followers.

When my father was in his twenties he fathered a child, a daughter, out of wedlock. He tried to marry the girl's mother, who had glimpsed my father's controlling ways and declared that she wouldn't marry him if he was the last man on earth. Instead of support from the parishioners at his mother's church, my father was whispered about and then finally shunned.

I felt a pang for my father—he was just a young man—and protective of his feelings. The disappointment he must have felt having Denice (that was his daughter's name) taken away from him and missing out on her life. I was disappointed, too; she was my half sister and I would never know her. Family was important to my father, and maybe this rending was why. I was angered by the insult, the injury, and the hypocrisy of a Christian congregation turning its back on him. My father stopped going to church and, according to my mother, never forgave them.

Forgiveness wasn't part of my father's way of thinking. Actions had consequences. He tried to control relationships with the threat of punishment and revenge. He wanted us to fight back, just not against him. Expressing anger wasn't encouraged or allowed. But that made it easier to merge my father's way of thinking with my teachers' at Redeemer, where I learned to turn the other cheek. To accept whatever was done to me and move on.

When Karen was killed, I kept the pain to myself. I didn't turn to God for comfort. I didn't ask God to help me, to make it easier. I wasn't angry with God, either. God hadn't pulled the trigger. Karen's murder was the result of the free will of a man. It was a choice to do wrong, to go against God's will. So I didn't ask God why. What was done was done. Unlike Lazarus, Karen wasn't coming back from the dead. The church, religion, God couldn't help me. I was on my own.

CHAPTER TEN

April 6, 1981

When I woke up Monday morning, the world was still spinning. I lay in bed and tried to feel Karen. To conjure up her spectral presence, the haunting soul that had visited me. I tried to coax her out with prayers and focused thoughts of *Please, please.* But the words disappeared like stones into the hollow of my sorrow. Karen's ghost was gone. The space in me that I wanted her to fill was larger now, harder to ignore.

I looked up at the ceiling and listened to my breathing. Ribbons of air threaded in through my nostrils, then knotted up in my chest. My arms and legs were numb. It was as though I had been thrown down a flight of stairs. I was broken and raw, like a burlap sack full of shattered glass.

Downstairs the kitchen fan churned sounds together—the pop of hot bacon grease in a pan with radio waves from 1010 WINS and the high-pitched whine of my father's electric razor. I stood in the doorway and watched my mother stomp around. Her robe flew open at the knees, the scent of Shalimar dusting powder swirled from her skin. A blue net held spongy pink curlers in place on her head. Her heels hung off the backs of worn-down house shoes. She bumped into the edges of things, out of sorts, annoyed by my hovering, bemoaning "how late it is already." She asked if I was still going to school. I was puzzled but—as with most things between my mother and my teenage self—it came out in a scowl. "Because of Karen," she said. "It's all right if you want to stay home." She looked at me when I didn't answer, tilted her head to the side. Annoyed and impatient.

Since kindergarten, I'd never missed a day of school. Not when I was sick with the flu or on crutches with a broken toe. Not when the increasingly baffling science classes made my head ache with panic. Not even when I was sure to do poorly on a test. I refused to cheat like the other kids; I was prepared to go down with honor. Always determined to do better next time.

I looked forward to the end of endless summer days. Of waiting for my parents to take me to the movies or the beach, of listening to the laughter of the neighborhood kids playing in the street, of enduring Billy's garage band down the block rehearsing "Smoke on the Water" in a never-ending loop.

Going back to school meant a new outfit and a new pair of shoes, new teachers, maybe even new friends. But most important, it meant new classes. I believed Mr. Farbstein, my ninth-grade science teacher, when he told us that the true purpose of life was to keep learning until the day we died.

If I didn't go to school because of Karen, I didn't know what else I would do.

I dressed quickly and didn't worry about how I looked. I pulled my frizzy hair back into two barrettes. I walked to the bus stop with my head bowed and watched the concrete underfoot. The sidewalk was unbroken, scored into perfect squares—though the farther I walked from home, the more cracks I could see. The shallow lines were thicker, went deeper. Entire sections were broken, crashed through by angry roots demanding attention and caution. At the bus stop whole chunks of cement were missing, exposing the darkest, blackest dirt underneath.

I slid into a seat on the Q2 bus and stared out the window. Thoughts of Karen tumbled heavily inside my head like wet clothes in a dryer. I saw her standing behind the counter, then facedown on the floor, then lying underneath a white sheet stained with blood.

I shut my eyes and reeled off the order of my classes instead. *Science, math, social studies, Spanish, English, band, gym.* I'd finished my homework on Friday night, before I found out Karen had been killed. Since then I hadn't thought about the assigned reading on World War II, the trigonometry theorems, the haunting of Heathcliff by Catherine on the moors. I wondered what Karen had been studying at her Catholic girls' school. Was she memorizing Bible verses like I had to at my Lutheran elementary school? The trip she was supposed to take to Spain was only weeks away. Would someone take her place? Would my aunt and uncle get their deposit back? Did they even care about the money? Karen had been killed over a mere $241. It was a gut punch, how her life had been ended. *Face blown off at point-blank range.* What did that even mean? How was that possible? Was there a nose, mouth, and eyes? Or just a bloody gaping hole? I flashed on photos of concentration camp victims from my social studies textbook. I didn't know how I would get through this day.

I got off the bus and plodded up the hill, surrounded by students. Black and brown kids mainly—Puerto Ricans and Dominicans, Filipinos—but also Asian and white kids, too.

I wondered if they had heard about Karen's murder. If Karen would be another Renee Katz, the seventeen-year-old Flushing girl pushed in front of an oncoming subway train. The screeching wheels severed her hand. A promising career as a classical flutist over before it began. The police never found the hooded Black man the media kept referring to as "the assailant." But everyone knew who Renee Katz was. She was in the papers and on the news just like Karen. Grandmaster Flash and the Furious Five immortalized her in a verse from "The Message": "*They pushed that girl in front of the train / Took her to the doctor, sewed her arm on again.*"

I thought if I had been on that subway platform, I would have saved her. I would have reached down and pulled her out of the path of the oncoming train. Or jumped onto the tracks and rolled us both under the platform as the train rumbled by. I would have chased down the assailant. Sprinted through the station after him and bolted up the stairs, tackled him to the sidewalk and held him down with my knee in his back.

My jaw clenched and my fingers balled into fists when I thought about stopping the assailant, the man—or maybe he was just a boy—before he had a chance to shove Renee Katz onto the track.

I would have protected Karen, too.

If I had been in the Burger King, I would have stopped the boy with the sawed-off shotgun. Snatched the gun right out of his hands and thrown it to the ground. Or better yet, pointed the barrel at his face, then racked a round into the chamber. He would have dropped to the ground, covered his head with two shaking hands while Karen called the police to come cart him off to jail.

But my daydream didn't make sense. I knew it was unlikely

that I would wrestle the shotgun away. That I would have been there in the first place. I would never have been in the Bronx, at that time of night, without my parents. I searched my brain for a scenario that put me there with Karen, one in which we were already best friends like I'd always wanted. But there was no way I could have saved her.

Jamaica High School loomed before me. It was a massive redbrick building with east and west wings, surrounded by a rolling green lawn and enclosed in a black iron fence. I walked past clusters of rock 'n' rollers. The kids who listened to Led Zeppelin, Pink Floyd, and the Who. They wore concert T-shirts and ripped jeans with bandanas dangling out of back pockets or tied around pimply foreheads, holding long, greasy hair out of their stoner-red eyes. They were unburdened by knapsacks full of textbooks and homework. Their only concession to the classroom was a pencil tucked behind an ear or nestled inside a pack of Marlboro Reds and rolled up in the short sleeve of a T-shirt.

I looked for the skinny girl with the painted-on jeans, spiked heels, and curly blond hair who everyone said was Christine Sixteen from the Kiss song. I recognized the stage crew boys from when I was in the school play. They ran the lights and sound, built the sets. They were friends with Kevin, the cute shaggy-brown-haired boy with a pug nose and baby seal eyes whom I had a crush on. By chance on my way to the bathroom one day I found out that we sat in the same seat during different classes. I started writing notes for him on the desktop. That ended when he found out who I was and left a note that said "I don't date niggers." Stung but not surprised, I scratched out our notes with pen. After that he started writing to another girl who sat there during a different period.

The disco kids were on the other side of the sidewalk. They wore shimmery nylon tops, tight polyester pants with polished pointy dress shoes. And that was just the boys. They gathered around the parked cars of the older bad-boy dropouts who blasted music from speakers in the trunk or carried suitcase-size boom boxes on their shoulders like dumbbells. The girls were tiny and teetered like praying mantises on too-high heels. Skinny purses on long metal chains bumped off their bony hips, threatening to knock them off balance as they talked, gesturing wildly with their hands and neck.

I saw Serena, the Puerto Rican girl who'd tried to be my friend. But one night on the phone she told me how much she hated niggers. When I reminded her I was Black, not Puerto Rican like she thought, she insisted that she knew. "I call everybody nigger," she said, laughing.

I walked quickly past her and inside the gate. I wanted to find my friends. I made my way down a long path to the flagpole right in front of the grand entrance to the school—a trio of arched dark metal double doors underneath an ominous bell tower. This was where the honors students gathered. A phantom breeze pushed the rope against the metal flagpole with a persistent sharp tap, like an outside guest knocking to come in. I moved through the crowd and joined my classmates.

Suddenly I was on the verge of tears. I wanted to talk to someone about Karen, the dead girl in the newspapers. Then I realized no one would know who she was to me. I wished the reporters had interviewed me, quoted me, the grieving cousin, the relative who aspired to be her best friend. I wanted people to know what I had lost. I felt sick to my stomach for thinking that way. For needing the attention. For wanting someone to ask. But I kept my eyes open for a sympathetic ear.

Wiry, wavy-haired Ben stood nearby. He could have been considered a class clown, but he was confident and his outbursts were too smart to be easily dismissed as just attention seeking. He listened quietly to a motley assortment of geeks, nerds, and bookworms. Their faces animated with tales from the weekend spent in Hebrew school and temple. Legs and feet tapping, they barely listened as they waited to breathlessly one-up one another, eager to spit out facts that everyone already knew. In the same conversation they'd discuss science projects, Billy Joel, and Israeli politics.

I moved on to Steve and Stephen: one was short and spry, sarcastic but sweet; the other was a sincere teddy bear, stocky with shaggy hair and glasses. I had crushes on both but had been advised that because I was a *shiksa*, a *goy*, and a *schwartza*, they'd never ask me out. And if they did, I'd be little more than practice until a nice Jewish girl came along. Only half the girls in my classes were Jewish. The rest were Chinese or whites who didn't want to be called that. They were Greek, Italian, Irish, Puerto Rican, Polish—and proudly so. The daughters of immigrants, they wore their ethnicity as a badge of honor, like their good grades and good behavior. They were my competition for our teachers' admiration and glowing letters of recommendation for college. I didn't want them to know about Karen.

I hid behind a flock of bohemian hippie-chicks. The ones with puka shell necklaces and long, straight hair that fell past the drawstrings on their gauzy peasant skirts. They mingled with the fashion plates, the sorta-smart, outgoing girls who dressed in designer blouses and name-brand jeans. The air crackled with their shrieks and cackles as they complimented this one's jewelry or the french braid in that one's hair.

I knew if I got too close they'd ask me about my weekend. If I told them the truth, they'd cover their mouths and shake their heads as they listened to the story of Karen's murder. They'd form a circle around me, rub my back, and say, "If there's anything I can do." By the end of the day, everyone in school would know. I'd be the subject of whispers and stolen looks. Pulled aside, apologized to, asked how was I doing. People I barely knew would call me at home. They'd insist on mourning with me. Then I'd have the burden of politely acknowledging their thoughts, prayers, and sympathy. Though some might have a hard time believing it and wonder what kind of a family I came from that a sixteen-year-old relative could be murdered at an after-school job. I felt the heat of sweat on my neck and tried to smooth down the frizz of my hair with the palm of my hand.

Lisa grabbed my raised elbow and wiggled it back and forth. "Hey, Slime," she said.

When we weren't calling each other Slime, we'd try Sleaze, occasionally Scuzz or Scuzzy. Silly nonsense nicknames that made us laugh and let everyone else know we were friends.

"How are you?" she asked. I could tell by the crinkle of concern around her eyes that she had read about Karen's murder in the newspapers. Over the weekend, articles about the investigation had come out in the *Post*, the *Times*, and the *Daily News*, which ran an old photo of Karen, with her curly hair and bright eyes.

I wasn't sure what would come out of my mouth if I tried to speak. I didn't want to cry. I nodded and managed a small smile that made me self-conscious as soon as it crossed my lips. Lisa squeezed my shoulder. "I am so, so sorry," she said, sounding like she had when I hadn't been cast in the school play. I bristled. She didn't understand. How could I explain that my hopes of having a real friend, a best friend even, had died with Karen?

"How was your weekend?" I changed the subject, then watched Lisa talking as my mind drifted and created images of things I knew but hadn't actually seen.

My mother told me that the night Karen was killed, my aunt and uncle had gone to the crime scene. Word had spread through the neighborhood about a robbery in which shots were fired and someone was killed. Her parents drove up to the end of the street where the Burger King was. A uniformed officer stood guard behind the yellow crime scene tape. He pointed to an ambulance speeding away and told my aunt and uncle that their daughter was being taken to the hospital. Aunt Barbara and Uncle Warren got back into their car and raced after the flashing lights and siren sounds to Misericordia General. They ignored the signs, parked haphazardly in a red zone, and ran after the paramedics rushing a stretcher with a patient they couldn't quite see into the emergency room. My uncle flashed his badge at the nurses' station and stepped through the fluttering nylon curtain wall of an examination room. There they caught sight of a dark brown–skinned foot hanging off the gurney and knew it was not their light-skinned daughter.

I was angry with that officer for sending my aunt and uncle on a wild-goose chase, for giving them false hope. But my father said that the officer was right not to let my aunt and uncle see their little girl "that way." He said, "They would have messed up that whole crime scene. Then what? She was already dead. No, he did the right thing."

Lisa shook my elbow again. "Earth to Slime. You going to

class?" The bell was finally ringing. My mother was right: I didn't want to be there.

The halls of my high school were decorated with ornately framed posters of famous works of art. *Guernica* and *The Starry Night. The Persistence of Memory.* Before social studies class, I stood opposite a framed reproduction of *The Last Judgment* by Hieronymus Bosch. I was drawn to this unnerving display of heinous crimes and human suffering. A reminder of the terrible things that would happen when you didn't follow the rules. Though following the rules hadn't helped Karen.

My classmate Carter walked up to me. He planted his elbow on the wall next to my head and smushed his cheek against the flat of his open palm. When he leaned in, I noticed the freckles across his nose and a slightly soapy scent in his blond hair, parted sharply on the side. As always, he was wearing his varsity baseball jacket and seemed on the verge of laughter.

Carter was quick with a joke, sarcastic comment, or off-color observation. He didn't take himself or anything too seriously.

"You do the homework?" he asked.

I wondered what he was after, then leveled him with a look. "Yes."

"Lemme copy it real quick."

"No."

"Why not?"

"Why should I?"

"Why shouldn't you?" He smiled. I pushed off the wall and lugged my book bag into the classroom.

"Everyone does it."

"So ask everyone," I said.

"I could just take it, you know," he called after me.

"Have some dignity," I said. "You should go down with honor."

Carter laughed out loud. "You are such a weirdo. What's the big deal? It's just homework."

It was more than just homework. I slid into my seat.

Carter stood over me with his arms crossed and a finger tapping his sleeve. I pointedly ignored him by slowly setting up everything I would need on top of my desk: textbook, spiral notebook, black pen and sharpened pencil lined up in a groove carved into the wood. I knew he was still watching when I squinted at Mrs. Riger's white chalk handwriting on the blackboard—a neat cursive, more angular than round. An adult's penmanship. Authoritative and decisive. She had written out questions about the end of World War I. I was about to write the questions down when Carter snatched the spiral with my homework off my desk.

He laughed at me over his shoulder and sped toward the front of the class. I leapt out of my chair and caught his sleeve in my left hand. He fell over, into a front-row seat, and dragged my spiral under the desk. I slapped at his lifted knees, holding me at bay.

"Just let me copy it."

"No," I said. "Never."

"Riger's coming."

"Give it back, Carter."

I lunged and snatched the soft green cardboard cover in my right fist. I tried to pull it away but Carter wouldn't let go. I tried yanking the notebook out of his hand. He leaned farther back, digging in for a game of tug-of-war, and dragged the bony top of my thumb across the splintered wood bottom of the desk.

The delicate skin caught on a piece of jagged metal that twisted my flesh open like the twirled top of a sardine can. I yelped as blood doused my hand. Carter slipped off the chair, halfway to the floor.

"Jesus," he said, clawing himself upright. "Are you okay?"

"Get away from me." I snatched my spiral out of his hand.

Mrs. Riger walked to her desk and looked around the room. "What's going on?"

I hadn't noticed that my classmates were frozen, watching.

"Nothing." Carter shrugged red-faced and sauntered to his assigned seat. But I couldn't move on.

"Carter tried to steal my homework." I waved the bloody spiral as proof.

The air surged with a burst of shocked laughter and surprise from my classmates.

"All right, people, settle down." I waited for Mrs. Riger to punish Carter. But she looked down at her textbook and flipped through the pages, as though she hadn't heard me.

Blood spilled out of the open wound and covered my fingers in a satiny glove. There was too much to suck clean. It dripped off my hand in perfect teardrops that splashed into stars on the floor. I tucked the spiral into my book bag, then fished around for the folded cotton handkerchief my father made me carry, and pressed it over my bleeding thumb. I felt light-headed, but I refused to sit down.

"Mrs. Riger, he stole my homework." She didn't look up. "You know, everyone cheats in your class. Even on tests. They share answers."

I heard agitated voices behind me.

"What is she doing?" someone hissed.

"Shut up."

Mrs. Riger pushed her glasses up with an index finger, rubbed the bridge of her nose, and sighed. "Thank you for telling me. I'll be on the lookout. Now let's everybody settle down. The bell is going to ring shortly." She turned her back on me to write on the blackboard.

The handkerchief was stained through with blood. My hand throbbed. I stumbled into the hallway and ran my thumb under the nearest drinking fountain. The clear water turned crimson and the wound stung like an angry bite. I didn't care about the bell or my homework or class anymore. I loped into the girls' bathroom for clean paper towels to stem the flow.

When I pushed on the door I was hit in the face by a gust of cold air from an open window. The bitter tang of smoke burned the hairs inside my nose. Christine Sixteen was perched on the windowsill, pointy-toed boots resting on the porcelain lip of a dirty old sink. She almost tossed her cigarette out the window until she realized I was nobody. She took a long drag, then passed the smoldering butt to a snaggletoothed, dark-haired friend, inspecting blackheads in the mirror with her nicotine-stained fingers.

I pulled rectangular sheets of rough folded white paper out of a silver dispenser.

"Oh, shit, what happened to your hand?"

"Carter . . . some boy tried to steal my homework. I wouldn't let him."

They looked at me, expecting more. Christine Sixteen shook her head. "Fucking brainiac. Well, good for you. Don't give up without a fight."

They smoked and watched as I struggled to cover my wound with the rough paper. Then Christine Sixteen said, "Here." She jumped to the floor, tucked the cigarette into the corner of her mouth, and squinted into the wisps of smoke, just like my mother. She took my hand in hers and turned her head, considering how to fix me.

Snaggletooth shook her head. "That ain't gonna work." She grabbed a roll of toilet paper from a stall and pressed a small stack of the rough paper towels, folded into quarters, over my bloody bone. Together they wrapped my hand like a trainer taping up a boxer before a bout. The gentle pressure of their attention was soothing.

"My cousin was killed this weekend."

They looked at me to see if it was true. "Yeah?"

"Yeah," I said.

"Shit."

"Yeah, sorry."

I nodded. Then the three of us watched silently as the layers of white wound round and round, covering my wound.

CHAPTER ELEVEN

April 6, 1981

When I got home from school I didn't bother to go up to my room. I abandoned my book bag on one of the high-backed chairs next to the stereo and slumped down in the middle of the couch—chin on my chest, hands tucked underneath my thighs, legs extended. The blinds had been drawn, anticipating night.

My mother sat at the desk where she wrote checks and paid the bills. There were newspapers in sections on the carpet around her feet. The New York *Daily News* was spread open, covering the clutter of office supplies, a daily calendar, and the ragged notepads that lived on top of the desk. In the ashtray a lit but unsmoked cigarette had smoldered down to the butt and turned into a delicate cylinder of gray nicotine lace. I could tell my mother had been crying.

She turned on the reading lamp. "It was an accident. The boys who killed Karen . . . one of them called the *Daily News*. He said it was an accident."

"It's in the paper?" I asked.

"Right here." My mother held up a corner of the flimsy newsprint for me to see. "They didn't mean to shoot her. Sweet Jesus."

I took the paper, skimmed it quickly until I saw the word. "Accident," I said out loud, trying to process this new information. Karen didn't have to die. The robbery should have been just another story, family lore retold with exaggerated details to the uninitiated at holiday gatherings or written into Karen's college application essay as an example of her resilience and resolve. If a good girl like Karen could be killed in an accident, then anything could happen. There seemed to be no point in listening to your parents or doing as you were told. No point to even trying.

My father came down from upstairs. His slippered feet trod heavily on the carpet-covered steps, making the wood underneath crack and moan beneath his weight. He was home early from work. A bath towel was cinched around his waist, beads of water clumping his hair into errant tufts and clinging to his naked chest and biceps. He reminded me of a boxer in the middle of a bout, dripping sweat. He'd showered, which meant he was going back out. I wondered if he was going to the Bronx and if he was still on the hunt for the killers now that we knew it was an accident.

"You have a cigarette, Mel?" He held out his hand and hovered, waiting for my mother to do what he wanted. My teeth clenched. I felt a rising enmity toward my father. He couldn't control what happened any more than Karen's parents could. Why did I listen to him? Why did my mother?

My mother sighed and reached down for her pocketbook. She pulled out tissues, a ziplock baggie full of loose mints and sugar-dusted sticks of gum, the folded program from a Sunday church service past, then laid them out on the newspaper. She found her cigarettes, in a white pack with a gold crown and a blue seal. They were a hard-to-find brand called Herbert

Tareyton, the original, unfiltered version of Tareyton, with the slogan "Tareyton smokers would rather fight than switch." Instead of putting it in his hand, she held one out for my father to take.

"Here," she said.

"Can I have two?"

"You may buy two. Yes." She pulled out a second cigarette.

My mother charged my father twenty-five cents every time he bummed a smoke. His brand was Pall Mall in the red pack, but he was always running out. Hers was expensive and hard to find. She charged him to borrow the car, too. This started after he told her he wasn't going to pay the monthly car note and insurance. Which was after she told him she was going back to work. My father didn't need the car to get to work. He took the subway or the Long Island Rail Road into Manhattan. She was the one who needed a car to commute to the schools out on the Island where she taught. But he forgot about visiting his mother on the weekend, trips to the hardware store, and getting back from the garden center with soil and mulch. She charged him by the hour, with a discount for half a day. She would pull out her composition notebook ledger and write it down in a running tab, then present him with an invoice at the end of the month.

This was my parents' marriage. An endless tit for tat, the constant threat of "I'll show you." He did what he wanted but tried to control her every move. She punished him for making rules. The first time he told her he wanted a divorce, her only question was "When?" The next time, she stopped buying swiss cheese, rye bread, coffee, half-and-half—all the foods he liked. When he noticed we had run out, she told him, "Nobody else in this house eats those things. You said you were leaving." The last time, she told him no, not until I was out of college. She said, "I'm not going to let you mess up that child's life."

My mother made my sister and me promise that if they ever did get divorced we would go with her. *But what about Daddy?* I thought, worried about what would happen to my father if he were alone. I'd heard it said a man without a family is a dangerous thing. Even with a family, my father was a caution. My mother knew this; maybe that's why she ended every criticism with a compliment. "He's a good father." "A good provider." "A good man." She always said she was happy to be married. "To have you kids."

My father was the only man my mother had ever been with. When my sister and I were old enough to know what those noises were coming from their bedroom, we giggled, then groaned with teenage disgust when it continued unabashed and unabated. My parents never walked anywhere together without holding hands. They said "I love you" and kissed instead of "Hello" and "See you later."

They eloped on December 2, 1952. He cleaned the gutters. She vacuumed the rugs. He put up storm windows in the winter. She hung the heavy drapes for fall. He planted tulips each spring. She cooked every meal. My father was in charge of everything outside the house. My mother took care of the inside.

"Are you okay?" my mother asked. She caught me staring at them, though my gaze had drifted inward to my thoughts. I nodded yes and watched her wipe away tears. My father hadn't cried again since that unguarded moment of raw pain when he'd first heard the news of Karen's murder. I wanted to know how he felt now that we knew it was an accident. I knew my father would rather talk about stock dividends and politics, Johnny Mathis and Nat King Cole, taxes, travel, and the land he owned upstate. When I was ten, I told him he needed to be saved to go to heaven—and he told me he didn't want to talk about that ever again. He talked about God being a woman, Jesus being Black, and Castro outlawing racism. Then he talked about whitey, the Jews, and niggers. He talked about how he felt, but not about his feelings.

My father lit his twenty-five-cent cigarette and stood in the light streaming in the front door window. He squinted through the smoke and looked outside at the houses across the street.

I thought that if he couldn't talk to me then, he never could. *If he can't talk to me now, I'll never listen to him again.* I asked, "How could they shoot her by accident?"

"Finger slipped. Gun had a hair trigger." He said this like I would know what that meant. Then he shook his head. "That's what happens." Confusion creased his forehead. I could see his thoughts were churning. The idea of it being an accident bothered him.

Once my father and two other parole officers chased a parolee out of his apartment, down to the street, and through a series of alleys that led into a dark courtyard in the heart of the projects. The parolee had a knife and wildly slashed the air. He sliced through one of the parole officers' coat sleeves, down to his skin. The parole officer drew his gun just as my father emerged, racing through a tunnel into the open night air of the courtyard.

"No, no!" he yelled at the parole officer whose gun was aimed and ready to fire at the knife-wielding parolee. "Stop, stop. It doesn't have to be like this. It doesn't have to end this way." My father stormed over to the parolee, snatched the knife away, and smacked the back of his head. "What's the matter with you? Do you want to die?"

My father's parolees were young men like Karen's killers. Angry and confused. Forever failing, full of excuses. These were the people he was paid to look after. They all said they wanted a better life. And it was my father's job to help them. My father said he could not rehabilitate someone who had never been habilitated in the first place. Still, he showed up every day—showered, suited up, strapped—and he tried. I was proud of him for that.

It was easier when Karen's killer was the sum total of his bad actions—a bad person who had done a very bad thing—and not the twenty-year-old air-conditioning-repair student who needed money so he thought to rob a fast-food joint. Not the damaged son, volatile brother, or wounded cousin of another family. It was easier when the killer was unknown. A monster. But no one is all good or all bad. We do the best that we can do. Even me, struggling not to be angry with my father. Trying to understand how the threat of violence that made my father seem strong was also his weakness.

I wanted to ask if he was still planning to kill the killers. All I got out was "What are you going to do now?"

"I'm going to the Bronx," he said, and then walked quickly up the stairs.

CHAPTER TWELVE

Thirty-three years later, Karen's murder was back in the news. On November 12, 2014, my mother called to tell me there was an article in the New York *Daily News* about Karen's killer coming up for parole. I wondered, with a sense of dread, if this meant the *Daily News* would publish an article every time the killer had a parole board hearing or only if he got out. Even though the *Daily News* had helped bring in one of the suspects, I still wondered who at the paper was keeping this story alive. Who else, besides family, was unable to let it go?

My mother promised to mail me the news article. It didn't occur to her that I could just pull it up online. There was a picture of Karen's Catholic schoolteacher looking both angry and sad, holding an old photo of Karen with her classmates. They were all sitting on the floor—some smiling, others laughing—all sprawled out on top of one another's laps. "I do beseech you to deny parole to Mr. Ramirez," the teacher pleaded in a handwritten letter to the parole board that the paper had photographed and put in a box next to the article.

Uncle Warren was quoted in the article as well. "They told us that any letter that comes in, they'll put it in the pile. All we can do is wait." I couldn't remember the last time I had seen Uncle Warren in person. I had no memory of him after Karen's funeral. He wasn't at the family gatherings I attended. He and Aunt Barbara had separated, though they never divorced.

I wondered if he knew whether or not my father had visited the parole board hearings for any of the boys who'd taken part in the Burger King robbery. I wanted to ask him, but I felt uncomfortable contacting a man I hadn't been in touch with for the last thirty-three years, to bring up his dead child. It was clear from his quote that Uncle Warren wanted the killer to stay behind bars. He wasn't alone.

According to the article, the parole board had been inundated with letters against granting parole. The hearing had been delayed six months due to the sheer volume of letters and an "outstanding litigation." It sounded as though Karen's killer had gotten into trouble in prison. Now I would have more time to research the young men who had killed Karen. To find out who they were then and now. I started by collecting all the newspaper articles on the case I could find.

An early article said the gunmen fired for no apparent reason. A subsequent article reported that the gunmen were "extremely nervous and on edge and didn't seem that familiar in handling guns." A policeman said, "It's very possible that the gun went off accidentally." Then a later article confirmed that a gunman with a Hispanic accent called the police on Saturday morning to say it was an accident.

From an article with the headline "Friends Mourn a Murder Victim, 16" I learned that a week before Karen was shot, she had told her close friends that she worried about her father because he was a city policeman in a city full of crime and violence. I found out that dozens of officers volunteered to work on Karen's case on their own time without pay. Karen had started working at the Burger King around Christmas vacation, "and she really seemed to enjoy it." One of the articles said, "Like thousands of other city teenagers, Miss Marsh worked part-time for pocket money and independence." The week after Karen was killed, she was supposed to go on a school trip to Europe, she was saving her money to spend on the trip. One of the articles quoted Aunt Lorin. She said that Aunt Barbara had hesitated when Karen asked if she could get a job. "We're a very close, careful family," the paper reported her saying. "When the kids want to go to a movie or to a dance, we'd always take them and pick them up. But we knew we couldn't ask the kids to live in a bubble."

Nine days after Karen was killed, the gunmen were in police custody. Two of the accomplices turned themselves in. Nineteen-year-old Luis Torres, who waited outside in a car during the robbery, turned himself in to the 46th Precinct station house in the Bronx. Twenty-year-old Francisco Alemar, who had gone inside the Burger King with a handgun and made the anonymous call to the police, turned himself in to the *Daily News*.

There was a picture of Francisco Alemar sitting at a table across from the reporter. He looked like a young Edward James Olmos. Head full of hair, glasses, wearing what looked like a puffy down jacket over a dark V-neck sweater, with a white collared shirt underneath. The white collar is what got to me. It jutted out from his sweater in sharp, straight lines and framed his neck and face with respectability, dignity. He didn't look like the monster I expected, maybe even hoped for. He looked professional, like an office worker or manager, not like someone who would carry a gun.

The article said he was in night school learning to be an air-conditioning technician. He had a job as a pleater in the Garment District of Manhattan, making $190 a week. A stone's throw away from the parole office where my father worked. Alemar said he took a pay cut of $40 to get an entry-level job in his field. He said, "It was worth it for a career in the future. Look what I have done to my future now." I wondered what kind of men they had become behind bars. What kind of men could they become, except for prisoners?

I thought of my father quoting his parolees: "Seemed like a good idea at the time." They brought the guns to scare the kids into doing what they wanted. To exercise some control they might otherwise not have had.

The article said the police were not surprised the men turned themselves in, because an unnamed confidential informant (CI) had identified the triggerman, Santiago Ramirez. Police seemed to imply that even without the CI they would have found the triggerman. He was the spitting image of the composite sketch.

The police tracked down Ramirez across the country. He had fled the state and was hiding out with his grandparents in Anaheim, California, home of Disneyland, the happiest place on earth and only an hour's drive from where I now lived. The article said Ramirez was "removed" from his grandparents' house by "a team of heavily armed FBI men." He was charged with second-degree murder and armed robbery.

The article went on to describe again what had happened the night Karen was killed. This time as I read, a detail caught my eye. One of the assailants was "said to have fired his shotgun twice as he fled." This was news to me. *Fired twice.* I'd never heard that before. I looked back through the other articles, and to my surprise they all mentioned the same thing, but somehow I had missed it. "Fired two blasts from a shotgun."

"Fired two shots." And perhaps the most disturbing description: "They were walking out when the robber carrying the shotgun abruptly turned and fired twice."

"Abruptly turned and fired twice" didn't sound like an accident to me. I didn't think it was possible to fire a shotgun twice accidentally. I'd learned how to shoot one while doing research for a TV show. As I remembered it, you had to chamber a shell in the shotgun before you fired, a deliberate motion that produces an unforgettable, threatening sound. It was hard enough to do it once, standing still, let alone twice, while moving, adrenaline pumping. Unless the shotgun was an automatic, but the article didn't specify the type of weapon it was. Even if it was an automatic, the gunman would still have had to pull the trigger intentionally a second time. So how did the shotgun go off accidentally twice? What had really happened that night? I was starting to think that maybe I didn't know the whole story.

CHAPTER THIRTEEN

April 7, 1981

I woke up Tuesday and thought, *Karen has been dead for four days.* The cut on my thumb was still raw, but a light scab had started to form. I ran my finger over it and considered picking off the thin layer of crystalline new skin, but didn't. I wanted to heal. I got ready for school but couldn't make it out of the house. My father had gone back to the Bronx the previous night. I could picture him and Uncle Warren cruising up and down the street, their faces framed by the front and rear passenger windows of some off-duty cop's car, scowling into the night. Ready to jump out and scoop up anybody who looked like he might know something about the boys who killed Karen.

The previous day's *New York Times* was still lying on the floor, folded over to the article with the headline "Police Seek 2 Gunmen Who Shot Teen-Agers in a Robbery in Bronx." I read it several times and tried to absorb the understated violence of the words. The gunmen had forced their way into the restaurant, then fired as the pair was leaving the shop. The article referred to Karen as "the dead girl." I read those words over and over. *Dead girl. Dead girl.* "Dead girl." I finally said it out loud and saw Karen's face smiling back at me from a memory.

The article said the gunman called the *Daily News* just before noon on Saturday to say it had been an accident. He wanted the world to know that he hadn't meant to kill the officer's daughter. He must have known the only thing worse than killing a cop was killing a cop's child. That meant that while my father and Uncle Warren were planning how to find and kill the gunman, the gunman was taking steps to make sure that he lived. I was chilled by the idea of either outcome.

I heard my mother moving around upstairs and put the paper away. I wanted to get out before she came downstairs and started asking questions I couldn't answer. Questions like "How are you?" The initial shock and adrenaline rush of Karen's murder had ebbed, leaving me suspended. Poised like an intake of breath waiting to be expelled. I quickly left the house to go to school.

The bus ride was a blur. When I stepped off onto Hillside Avenue, I couldn't remember how I'd gotten there or what I'd been thinking about as I made my way. I walked all the way up the hill without noticing the steep incline or the weight of my book bag. I ambled past the rock 'n' rollers hugging the fence and the disco dancers perched on cars. Christine Sixteen tossed me a head nod with a crooked little smile. I tossed one back and slipped into a corner behind a concrete balustrade near the front entrance. I hid from Lisa and turned away from the other kids in my classes. I repeated the order of my schedule in my head—*science, math, social studies, Spanish, English, band, gym.*

I looked down and fixed my gaze on the top of my reddish-brown book bag. For the first time in my life I had not done my homework. I didn't know what happened when you didn't do the work. It occurred to me that I should have been worried or panicked, full of regret or dread, but I wasn't. The rules I normally adhered to, the code of conduct I lived by, didn't apply anymore.

I opened my science text and tried to read about blast waves, bursts of energy that pulled fire and oxygen away from a fuel source and created a negative space, a stillness, a vacuum, that was destined to explode. Karen's sudden, violent departure from this world had left a negative space inside me. I knew nature abhorred a vacuum and that this space was likely to be filled by something. I didn't know what.

I got away with sitting quietly and saying nothing through science and math. I was surprised by how easy it was. With two periods down and five to go, I walked into social studies and saw Mrs. Riger writing questions on the blackboard. I took my seat and sat back as students streamed in, flooding the aisles with laughter and conversation. Someone opened a window, and a light breeze kissed cool air across my cheek. I turned my head and breathed it in. What I needed was a daydream—about a boy, about the summer, about going to college. I closed my eyes, but there was nothing behind my lids. No pictures, no images. No light at all. A murky nothingness was before me.

"Open your textbooks," Mrs. Riger said. We were studying World War II and the rise of the Nazi Party. I buried my gaze in the textbook's shiny pages, bright with reflected light. I didn't want to be called on to talk about pogroms, the invasion of Poland, or the Warsaw Ghetto. I didn't know how to make sense of events I hadn't witnessed. I tried to grasp the cumulative effect of individual incidents. How, one by one, each added up to a groundswell of change that led to a war. My head couldn't comprehend, but I had a visceral reaction to the black-and-white pictures in the textbook.

Travelers in winter coats with suitcases lined up against a brick wall. Confusion on their faces, they looked into the camera, haunted. Armed soldiers dotted the near distance. I felt a lump in my throat, then turned the page. Skeletal bodies with bulbous shaved heads, naked in a waterless shower. Bones jutted out of saggy, wrinkled skin—knobby knees and rows of ribs. Then gaunt faces with sunken cheeks, swallowed by oversize black-striped pajamas. Some leaned propped up on elbows in wooden summer camp–like bunk beds except without the sleeping bags or care packages from home. They had rictus smiles and dead black eyes, hollowed from desperation and despair. Innocence lost and murder on display. My stomach turned. Anger flared. Who was taking these pictures? The body destroyed. Whole lives reduced to parts; rooms piled full of human bones, teeth, or hair.

Mrs. Riger said, "We're going to go over last night's reading. Then we'll answer the homework questions from the end of the chapter together. This is too important to miss."

I suspected the mostly Jewish kids in my class already knew this history. A usual topic of discussion at family gatherings and Friday-night Shabbat. Where personal histories intertwined with world events and were passed down from generation to generation, to be absorbed into the psyche of each soul. As familiar to them as stories about the Tuskegee Airmen, Malcolm X, and the Black Wall Street of Tulsa, Oklahoma, were to me.

"How does something like this happen? Hmmm? How does a man like Hitler come to power?" Mrs. Riger looked out over the classroom. Half a dozen kids waved their hands in the air, desperate to be the first to say out loud the answers they all already knew.

Mrs. Riger called on a boy with nerdy glasses, long, shaggy hippie hair, and a jock's physique. He twisted his body open to the rest of the room so everyone could hear. "They were swept up in the tide. They believed they belonged to the master race. Because they were blond-haired, blue-eyed—like Carter," he said and smiled, and everybody laughed.

"Me?" Carter raised his eyebrows, grinned with mock horror at the joking suggestion that he was a Nazi. "What about Betsy?" Carter pointed to the prettiest silken-blond-haired, sky-blue-eyed girl in the class. Her fair-skinned chin and cheek propped up on her index finger and thumb like a decorative plate on display. She twirled a pen around the fingers on her other hand and said, "I'm a good Jewish girl." The class laughed approvingly.

"And what about the soldiers?" Mrs. Riger asked. "How could they do this? How did they justify such behavior?"

Mrs. Riger called on me when I raised my hand. "Maybe they didn't know."

"Didn't know what?" Mrs. Riger asked. She cocked her head to the side with the hint of a challenge in her voice.

I felt a flush of heat rise from my chest to my cheeks. My breath shortened slightly at having to explain. "Maybe the soldiers didn't know people were being killed."

The room got very still.

"All right." Mrs. Riger hesitated, considering how to proceed. "How could they not know?"

"They were young. They were teenagers, right? The soldiers. Just boys."

"But soldiers. Still."

I felt the invisible weight of thirty pairs of eyes pressing down on me. I tried to explain.

"Yeah, but that doesn't mean they wanted to kill people. I mean, yes, they killed people. But I don't think they meant to kill people. That's all."

"So," she said, "you're saying they were just following orders?"

I didn't know what I was saying. I needed to believe that the Nazi soldiers didn't know what they were doing. That the world was safe and the Holocaust was just one big accident that wasn't supposed to happen.

"Yes," I said, hoping to stop Mrs. Riger from asking me more questions. "The soldiers were just following orders."

"I don't believe what I'm hearing." A voice was raised from the back of the room. Seats creaked as bodies shifted for a better look at Ben. He was practically standing on his desk in the last row, he was so agitated. In the very last seat, sitting on the back of his chair.

"Seriously. That's the stupidest thing I've ever heard." A derisive laugh caught at the back of the throat; his voice cracked. "Those soldiers knew what they were doing. Of course they knew."

I couldn't look at him, but I couldn't stop explaining. "No, they didn't. They couldn't have known what they were doing. They were young, just teenage boys—"

He laughed, incredulous. "Oh my God—"

I shook my head no, insisted, "They didn't know."

"Look," Ben said, pointing a finger at me from across the room. "My grandmother was in Dachau. She has a tattoo on her arm. Her brother and mother and father were all killed. She's the only one who survived. She had to watch as her whole family was marched to their death inside a train car. So don't sit there and tell me that the Nazis didn't know what they were doing. They knew. They knew."

"They didn't know. They didn't." *It was an accident.* I felt dizzy and cold. My stomach clenched. I doubled over. "I'm sorry." I grabbed the handle of my book bag and bounded out of my seat. I careened clumsily down the aisle, pawed the back door open, and ran out into the empty hallway. I stopped to catch my breath, then burst into tears. I had to keep moving. Instead of heading to Spanish, my next class, I darted into the first stairwell I saw. I dashed down the steps, past the cafeteria landing to a subbasement floor that dead-ended at a wooden double door, chained closed with a padlock. I eased down on the bottom step and looked out the small windowpanes in the door. Outside was a city park beyond the school gate. It was wooded, unkempt, and overgrown. Dangerous, with a crooked, broken path and busted-up, graffiti-covered benches. I caught my breath and let the tears flow freely. Then the bell rang. Kids thundered down the stairs, stomped into the cafeteria behind me. One of the rock 'n' roll boys walked past me, removed the opened padlock from the chain, pushed open the wooden doors, and, to my surprise, strode outside, past the gates, like it was nothing. The chain clanked off the metal door handle and coiled onto the floor like a snake. A handful of other kids soon followed him out. I watched them drift down the sidewalk into the adjoining neighborhood and disappear into the park.

I thought about walking out with them. And I didn't know where I would go. I didn't know the world beyond the school grounds. I had been told not to leave, and so I never had. But that day, the black gate surrounding the building was less like a barrier and more like the border to an unexplored world. I didn't leave. I wasn't free—I still had Spanish, English, band, and gym. I picked up the metal chain and dragged it around the door handle, then snapped the padlock closed. *Rules. Order. Safety.* I went to the rest of my classes.

Ben was waiting for me after school.

I saw him standing by the flagpole, sweatshirt draped limply over the crook of his arm, small duffel collapsed in a puddle at his feet. He was watching kids come out of the building. I was worried he was looking for me, so I walked quickly toward the gate.

"Hey—" Ben called out and came after me. I walked faster, determined to get away, yet steeling myself for a lecture, another round of being called stupid that I decided was best to endure without responding, to save face and dignity.

"Wait—" Ben yelled. "Stop." He caught up to me and tugged my elbow. "I want to talk to you." I turned slowly to face him.

"Mrs. Riger told us. About your cousin." I was surprised Mrs. Riger knew. I realized my parents must have told the school. That my classmates knew made me want to run and hide. "I read about the murder in the paper. I didn't realize that was your cousin." He looked at me with pity in his eyes. I put a smile on my face and held it there like a mask.

"I'm sorry. And I'm sorry I yelled at you. I didn't know. Why didn't you say something?" Tears pushed into the corners of my eyes. I shrugged and shook my head.

"Come on, I'll walk with you."

Ben put his hand on my back to reassure me. The warmth of his touch made me uncomfortable. I was glad that he knew, even though I felt embarrassed and exposed. I didn't want to be pitied. I didn't know what to say. We walked down the hill in silence. I kept my eyes on the gray sidewalk as I walked. I could feel Ben looking over at me.

"You know, you and I have known each other since freshman

year. There are only a few of us like that." He meant the kids who'd started at Jamaica in the ninth grade instead of the tenth.

"I know."

He counted them off on his fingers. "David, Dorothy, Karen. Stephen. Barbara. You should come hang out with us."

"Yeah, okay," I said. I could tell Ben had more on his mind.

"I just want you to know, I think of you as a friend. I mean, we're friends. And you can talk to me. Any time. Whenever you want. Okay?"

"Okay," I said, more because I knew he wanted me to than because I agreed.

"And we should do something. You know, hang out after school sometime."

I stopped at the bus stop.

"This you?" he said, checking the signpost. "Q2?"

"Q2. That's me."

"Cool. Okay, well . . . I'm sorry about today. I really am. And I'm sorry about your cousin."

"Thanks," I said, not sure what I was thanking him for exactly.

"I want you and me to be better friends." He smiled. Uncertain, I smiled back.

"Talk to you tomorrow?" He raised his eyebrows and pointed at me, his index finger frozen in place, waiting for an answer.

"Yes. Tomorrow."

"Okay, then." He nodded as if something had been decided between us. "See you later."

"Bye, Ben." I watched him walk back up the hill. My stomach churned.

From then on I would have to avoid Ben. I would have to

skate around his invitations and come up with excuses. I would have to pretend we were going to hang out, knowing we never would. We never could. I couldn't be friends with Ben.

My parents would never let me hang out with Ben. They'd make it difficult. I wouldn't be allowed to take public transportation to his house. They'd have to drive me there. Then find something to do nearby while they waited to bring me home. They would be annoyed at having to make small talk, at being forced to interact with his folks. I knew what they would say. "We don't have time for this nonsense. Can't you see him at school?"

It wouldn't have been any easier for Ben to come over to my house, either. My parents didn't like company. Especially strangers. They didn't want people "knowing our business." There were sensitive papers—bank statements and bills—all over the house that would have to be put away before anyone could come over. My mother would feel compelled to clean—straighten, dust, vacuum, and polish—every room, on every floor, even though we probably wouldn't be allowed to leave the living room. She wouldn't let us use the basement, where all her school stuff was and where my father had a workbench with expensive and dangerous tools that he didn't want anyone "messing around with." But my father wouldn't want us in the living room, either, where he had guns hidden in the bookshelf behind the World Book Encyclopedias and the hardbound book of poetry. "Why does he want to be friends with you, anyway?" my father would ask. He would say there was only one thing a little white boy, a Jewish boy from Jamaica Estates, could want from a sixteen-year-old Black girl, and it wasn't friendship.

But the main reason I couldn't be friends with Ben was because I didn't know how. Controlled and sheltered by my parents, I didn't want Ben to know all the things I knew nothing about: music, politics, parties, dating, sex, drugs, the world. Life. I felt nauseated. This was my father's fault. He said that people lie. He said "Better safe than sorry." He said I was a Black girl in a white world, and I had to be careful always. No one would understand my father's mistrust and paranoia. And I couldn't explain, didn't want to explain. The only person who would have understood was Karen. Karen was like me, raised like me, looked like me. It would have been easy to hang out with Karen. I could have been friends with Karen. I would have been friends with Karen. But Karen was gone and I was on my own.

CHAPTER FOURTEEN

Santiago Ramirez's parole board hearing had been postponed. I was still waiting for copies of his hearing transcripts. I wanted more information before I wrote a letter to the parole board. It occurred to me that the transcript from the criminal trial would also contain details about what had happened the night of the robbery. I would be able to find out if the shooting had been an accident. And if Ramirez really had fired twice.

It was still too early to call the Bronx courthouse. I tried to write. I had a script due. I was staffed on an MTV show about teenagers, tasked with telling stories about prom dates and pregnancy scares. My bread and butter was writing for cop shows and crime procedurals, so writing a soapy teen drama was a departure for me. But I wanted the challenge. As luck would have it, I was assigned the episode in which one of the beloved recurring characters would be accidentally killed in a robbery gone awry at the convenience store where he worked. I knew exactly how to write this. I sat with the details of how the character would be killed. Staging the stunt, and, more important, unraveling the emotions behind every moment, every terrifying second of that unfortunate event. I'd had to write scenes like this before, about victims of violent crime and the criminals who commit them. I found I could always picture the incidents clearly and would play them out in my mind's eye. Not just the external staging and required stunts, but the internal emotion—the panic, turmoil, and adrenaline rush. The ensuing trauma. For me, the emotion of these scenes was always just beneath the surface, readily accessible, though not cathartic. I got lost in the retelling. When I looked up, I saw the blue blush of first light. It was well past nine on the East Coast.

I called the Bronx County Hall of Justice and spoke with one of the court reporters. The woman was abrupt. She gave clipped, one-word answers to my rambling questions. Once she realized I was a relative of the victim, her tone softened. She apologized when she cautioned that it might cost as much as five hundred dollars for a copy of the trial transcript. I told her I was willing to pay and waited while she searched a database on her computer. Her acrylic nails clacked softly on the keys as she typed. "Humph," she said, before delivering the bad news. There was a flood in the eighties, many courthouse records were destroyed. She doubted a transcript from 1981 . . . "Oh, wait," she said, "I found something." Seconds later, a document appeared in my email inbox. A transcript of the sentencing hearing for Santiago Ramirez.

I printed out the transcript but couldn't calm down enough to read it. I placed the pages on the dining room table then paced around, hands on my hips, head cast down. A jumble of feelings in my stomach bubbled up into my chest, caught in my throat until I felt like crying. I wished I had a boyfriend, someone to comfort me, to help me understand why after thirty-three years I still couldn't come close to thinking about Karen's murder without being on the verge of tears. Why was it that the trauma of this loss wouldn't go away? A thick layer of sadness descended. Everything in my body, movements and thoughts, slowed to a buzzy stillness as I turned the events over in my head. What was I searching for? A moment when the outcome might have been different? I knew that could never be. A way to forgive? Not only the boys who did this, but myself? There was nothing I could have done to prevent Karen from being killed. Caught up in the loop of memory and emotion was something more than grief and sadness. Something unsettled that I couldn't identify. Unknown and unnamable.

I picked up the transcript, thumbed through the pages, and caught the words "Depraved indifference to human life." I was afraid to continue. I lingered on the cover page, drawn to the words "The People of the State of New York against Santiago Ramirez, defendant."

I'd never been to that particular courthouse in the Bronx, but I could easily imagine what the courtroom looked like. A cavernous rectangular chamber with high ceilings that still managed to feel tight and claustrophobic. Dark wood walls and low partitions, benches and desks that pulled your gaze from the airy, open space overhead down to the ground. There was something church-like about the layout of a courtroom, with its gallery of onlookers instead of congregants in pews, a jury box where the choir would be, and a black-robed judge at the altar presiding over sinners and those sinned against. In both church and court, the proceedings are about the human soul. Innocence versus guilt, punishment versus forgiveness, rules versus free will.

The rules of the court said that before the sentence was read, the People, represented by an assistant district attorney, had their say, then the defense attorney, and then the defendant. Finally, the judge would announce the sentence. But the straightforward orderliness of the sentencing hearing belied the intensity of the underlying process to determine how much prison time the convicted would serve.

The sentence is a result of several weeks of investigation into the crime and criminality of the convicted. Judges, however, don't conduct the actual investigation. That's delegated to a probation officer, who can take anywhere from four to eight weeks to write up a narrative about the convicted called the presentencing investigation, or PSI. The rules have since changed, but in 1981, probation officers were allowed to reinterview witnesses and question anyone they deemed useful to determining a sentence for the convicted, from a kindergarten teacher to a next-door neighbor at an old address. The process even allowed probation officers to interview witnesses who weren't allowed to testify during the trial.

The only reason I knew so much about the sentencing process and the presentencing investigation report was because I'd learned about it while writing cop shows. It sounded like a good idea for a television series. I'd started researching, and as with all things law enforcement, I'd asked my father if he could recommend someone I could talk to who did this job. He chuckled and said, "Yeah, your aunt—Barbara." I thought about that as I held the sentencing transcript in my hand. Years later I would find out that generating this report was not part of Aunt Barbara's job as a probation officer. But at the time it struck me as a cruel irony that Aunt Barbara might have been tasked with coming up with the sentence for convicted murderers. I imagined it must have been painful for her to keep doing that job after Karen was killed. But she did. She found a way to continue. I sat down at my dining room table and read the transcript.

The hearing began with the court clerk restating the conviction. Santiago Ramirez was found guilty of murder and assault in the second degree. In the transcript, the court clerk used the word "You." She spoke directly to the defendant. I felt a jolt. He was there. Of course he was there. But this was the closest I had ever been to Karen's killer. A man I had never met or seen. I didn't know what he looked like or sounded like. The hearing had taken place more than three decades earlier, and yet I felt his presence across time and space, through words printed on a page. It was electric, dangerous. To me, this young man was a threat, someone to be feared.

In the transcript, the assistant district attorney called the defendant "a mad-dog killer," barren of any sense of dignity for human life, devoid of any redeeming quality that would warrant a sentence of less than the maximum. The assistant district attorney described how earlier in the evening, before Karen was killed, Santiago Ramirez had sat in Devoe Park in the Bronx with his girlfriend and talked about the robbery that ended up taking Karen's life. The defendant's mother was sitting with them, though it is unclear whether she heard her son talk about the robbery that his girlfriend unsuccessfully tried to convince him not to commit. The ADA continued, "And even after he took her life, this defendant coolly, calmly unloaded and reloaded that shotgun with the presence of mind that clearly shows what kind of person he really is."

I wondered if "unloaded and reloaded" was a reference to the second shot and proof that Ramirez had indeed fired twice—although the transcript didn't actually say. Had Ramirez reloaded intentionally or as a reflex, unthinkingly racking the gun again, thereby moving another shell into the chamber? I didn't have a transcript of the trial testimony to know what witnesses had said happened. And the shotgun was never recovered, so I didn't know enough about the type of shotgun used to hazard an educated guess as to how it was loaded.

Later, the transcript showed the judge agreed that this action by the defendant presented a problem. "It seems to me that a man who has accidentally shot the top of the head of a 16 year old girl off accidentally, would probably, I may be in error, would probably drop that shotgun and run out screaming but we didn't have the situation here. . . . That caused me to have second thoughts as to whether or not there was an actual accidental shooting and it was most disturbing." I was disturbed as well. It occurred to me that the newspaper articles must have assumed there was a second shot because of the unloading and reloading, but maybe he never fired what he reloaded. According to the sentencing transcript, there didn't seem to have been a second discharge.

The moment when the shotgun was reloaded constituted the crux of the five-week trial. I didn't understand why there had even been a trial, when saying Karen's murder was an accident seemed like an admission of guilt. But the grand jury hadn't indicted on a murder charge, only felony murder, which was attached to the charge of robbery. There was no question the robbery had taken place, the defendant had admitted to that, but he'd pled not guilty on the grounds that he did not intend to kill Karen or anyone. Reloading the shotgun was thus a crucial moment, the linchpin that proved that the defendant was guilty, depraved and indifferent to human life, and not merely clumsy. That moment also now formed the linchpin to shaping my opinion of the defendant as someone who thirty-three years later didn't deserve to be forgiven or paroled.

Even at this late stage of the process, the defense attorney tried everything he could to reduce his client's prison sentence. He tried to paint a picture of his client as full of remorse and regret, insisting it had been an accident. Then he blamed the light trigger on the gun. "It was the unfortunate touching of the trigger which caused the firing, not a pressing or a squeezing of the trigger, but touching of a trigger which was exceptionally light, a light trigger, three to four pounds, as opposed to ten to 14 pounds for a normal gun." He harped on the grand jury's decision not to indict on murder as a factor that should mitigate the sentence. He called into question the instructions to the jury, then nitpicked the wording of the conviction. He argued that his client should serve only as much time as the accomplices, who'd each taken a plea and gotten only fifteen years to life. Then he pointed out that his client had never been in trouble before, that this—murdering Karen—was his first brush with the law. He offered as an excuse the reason for the robbery: the defendant needed money to pay a fine. I was so angry reading the litany of excuses that my hands trembled and I had to put the pages down.

And angrier still at his mother, father, aunt, cousins, and friends who had been there in the courtroom, lending their support. Karen meant nothing to them. *Depraved indifference to human life.* I wanted them to suffer the way Karen's mother, father, aunts, uncles, and cousins had. As the assistant DA had said in his statement, why should the defendant's family members get their loved one back when Karen was gone "beyond the veil [*sic*] of tears?" He used the seasons as a metaphor for the tragedy of Karen's murder. Instead of being in spring, a time of hope, joy, and new life, we were in the cold of winter, the season of loss, "for Karen Marsh is dead." Brutally murdered by a brazen defendant who hatched an "evil plan."

The robbery was premeditated. This was the first time it

had occurred to me that Santiago Ramirez didn't just walk into the Burger King by accident. He'd targeted that Burger King. Maybe he had even seen Karen behind the counter or, worse, been served by her when he scoped out the place. I didn't know if this was true, but I felt nauseated at the idea. *Depraved indifference to human life.*

When it was the defendant's time to address the court, he couldn't. He tried reading from a prepared written statement, but his nerves failed and his voice faltered. The court reporter asked him to speak up. The judge responded in a way that made me angry. He was solicitous: "Take your time, take your time and read it slowly. And I'll listen to you." The defense attorney had to read the statement for him.

The trial was an ordeal for the defendant, he claimed. He had tried to remain peaceful and calm despite what the ADA "made me look like." He felt discriminated against because of all the publicity surrounding the case. "It seems like I am accused of killing a New York City detective, not his daughter," he said. He called the judicial system "corrupt," "pathetic," and "designed to soil good people." He said, "This case was not proved beyond a reasonable doubt." I couldn't help but laugh at how ridiculous he sounded. I was disgusted, offended, and yet drawn to his words.

I reread the sentences in disbelief to make sure I was understanding them correctly, getting this right. And then I dissected his word choices, looking for some deeper meaning, the subconscious tells they revealed. He'd said, "I assure you, I will not be a victim." A victim for being on trial? A victim of whatever sentence was imposed? The defiance in the phrase "I assure you" felt like a threat. A promise that he would not be controlled or cowed in the future. Certainly this was not someone who should be let out on parole.

He referred to the reloading of the shotgun as "unusual behavior," something the prosecutor exaggerated. He wrote, "I am not a monster." Then he wrote it again: "I am not a monster."

He didn't apologize for what he had done. He didn't say it was an accident. He didn't wish that he could have changed the outcome of his actions, his depraved indifference to human life, except maybe for himself. "How can you put a man behind bars for a long period of time, 'specially when he hasn't been on this earth, planet Earth, for that long? I was proven guilty but two wrongs doesn't make one right. I am not asking for your sympathy, just another chance at life."

This was not someone full of remorse and regret, except for the loss of his own freedom. Still, his despair and desperation were palpable. I was surprised to feel my anger and sadness extending into compassion for this nineteen-year-old kid who was about to lose his life as effectively as Karen had lost hers. My chest tightened, and I could almost feel the closeness of the prison cell where he would spend the next three decades. Who wouldn't be scared and panicked by the impending loss of freedom, the prospect of being trapped? He had killed my cousin, yet somehow I felt sorry for him. In this last desperate plea for mercy, he wasn't a monster, just some stupid kid who had made a horrible mistake. To think he had never committed a crime before, and his first time out, this was what had happened. The last line of his statement spoke to me across the chasm of the decades gone by. *Another chance at life.* I still didn't know if he deserved it. I couldn't reconcile his reloading of the shotgun. But I had an idea who he had been. I needed to find out who he had become.

CHAPTER FIFTEEN

April 9, 1981

It was a closed-casket funeral. My mother warned me the mortician couldn't put Karen's face back together after the shotgun blast. For the service Aunt Barbara displayed a framed photograph of Karen smiling and draped a purple sweatshirt over the shiny white coffin.

I felt like I was inside a kaleidoscope: every fractured moment moved like a sharp shape shifting through a tube in diffused light. Recognizable, yet strange.

Mourners on the sidewalk spilled into the street, stood shoulder to shoulder against the back wall inside Trinity Baptist Church. Karen had gone to a Catholic school, but Trinity Baptist was her home church. The pews were packed with bodies, but the soaring ceiling made the sanctuary feel light and airy. Instead of black, the mourners wore purple. Instead of old, the grieving were young—Karen's classmates and friends.

My heart ached with a yearning to see Karen one last time, before they put her body into the ground forever. But I would never see my cousin again. My chest pulled tight with regret that the week before, I'd decided to stay home, to study for the SATs, instead of going with my father to the Bronx. "Karen will be there," he had said, trying to entice me. Now all I wanted to do was open the lid of the coffin for one last look. I opened the program instead.

I counted twenty items in the order of service. The invocation, the doxology, the Gloria, the message. The Lord's Prayer, a prayer of comfort, and three types of hymns—for trust, preparation, and parting. I knew them all by title: "Jesus Loves Me," "He Leadeth Me," "This Is My Father's World." I could hear their melodies before they were sung. The words sat ready on my tongue, but when the time came, the songs dropped out of my mouth a cold comfort. The lyrics were a cruel reminder to trust in God in troubled times.

This is my Father's world.
O let me ne'er forget.
That though the wrong
seems oft so strong,
God is the ruler yet.

Karen is dead, but God is still in charge. Blind faith. But I started to wonder why. Why had this happened? Was there a reason? A purpose for Karen's murder in God's bigger plan? The words of the reverend put that idea into my head.

The reverend didn't talk about how Karen had died. He didn't mention that she had been killed, murdered. Just that we should go on stronger and better so her "passing" would not be in vain. As if something good could still come of this.

At the end of the service the organist played the Funeral March by Chopin. The maudlin opening melody seemed cruel and absurd. The lyrics "*Pray for the dead and the dead will pray for you*" ran through my head as I remembered hearing this while watching Saturday-morning cartoons when I was a kid.

Everyone in the church filed out quickly, eager to get to the cemetery for the interment. My father complained that it was an hour's drive away, in Valhalla, New York. He didn't understand why they would bury her so far from the family. I didn't understand why he didn't want to go. I wanted to be there for every last minute of Karen's last minutes with the living, even though she was dead. I wanted to see where Karen's final resting place would be. I wanted to watch the casket being lowered into the ground. I wanted to watch the dirt cover it up until it was part of the earth and somehow connected to my feet. My father wanted to go home.

Outside the church, everything was in motion. Cars pulled out from the curb, glided into the procession behind the hearse. People walked in every direction. Wiped away tears. Cried into their hands. I saw the girls from Karen's class in their school uniforms looking lost, holding one another, anxiously chewing their hair or twirling strands of it around their fingers. I tried to figure out if they were sadder than me. I wondered if they knew Karen better than I did. My father left to get the car. I lost track of my mother. I was by myself, swept up in the tide of people, tumbling around like a seashell underwater. I landed on the sidewalk outside Aunt Barbara's house. For a while my cousin Warren and David, the white boy from Karen's sweet sixteen, stood with me. We watched the funeral procession. A seemingly endless line of cars streaming by, headlights on, en route to Valhalla.

There were so many cars it was unbelievable at first. Then ridiculous. And finally funny. I laughed out loud at how long the procession of vehicles lasted. They streamed by me in a blur of metal and glass. I stopped counting after fifty and grew annoyed.

How could there be this many people going to see Karen buried? A hollowness crept into my belly. I felt sick. Disgusted by the spectacle, the public display of grief. Did all those people really know and love Karen? Or were they just glomming on to the grief? Swept up in the moment by mourning? I watched with my mouth hanging open, eyes cast up, as cars crested the hill, then drove down the block.

It made no sense. None of it. Karen had been killed for no reason. No purpose. No greater calling. No bigger plan. She was not in heaven. She had not been called home. She had not gone to a better place. She was in a casket about to be put into the ground and covered with dirt. Everything I'd learned in church, in Christian school, it wasn't a lie; it just wasn't the truth. There was only one explanation that made sense of my pain, suffering, and questioning. I felt the answer first. It lighted on my skin, sank into my bones, and filled my mind with the peace of truth revealed. Then I heard a voice inside my head, one with an answer to the question of why this had happened. When I heard it, I felt free. I knew that from then on, everything was up to me.

The voice inside me said, *There is no God.*

CHAPTER SIXTEEN

After several phone calls to the Bronx criminal court, I found out that the transcript of the criminal trial was missing, most likely destroyed by a flood in the late eighties. But there was a transcript from the pretrial hearing motions. The original had been typed on onionskin paper, a paper so thin it could not be put through a copy machine, except by hand, one page at a time. My sister helped me hire someone in New York to scan each delicate page—897 pages in all—then email it all to me. I skimmed through the pages as they rolled off my printer. The hearing covered motions brought by the defense regarding the handling of evidence in a way that might be more helpful to his client. Like excluding the defendant's confession and other subsequent spontaneous utterances to law enforcement officers that confirmed his guilt, or not showing the jury a videotape of the crime scene that included Karen's lifeless body on the ground. I put the pages into two five-inch D-ring binders and read them over and over, trying to piece together exactly what had happened in the aftermath of the robbery.

CHAMBERS BAR WAS A favorite watering hole in the predominantly Irish neighborhood of Upper Manhattan known as Inwood. Katherine Kupper was at Chambers sometime between midnight and four or five a.m. on Sunday, April 12. Ms. Kupper told a member—possibly retired—of the NYPD that she knew details of what had happened in that Burger King in the Bronx the night that girl, the detective's daughter, was killed. This member of the NYPD—possibly retired—called the Manhattan night watch, as it was known, and officers responded to the location of Chambers Bar. They spoke with Ms. Kupper, then transported her to the Bronx Detective Task Force office in the 48th Precinct, where she became an unofficial confidential informant, or CI. "Unofficial" because the detective didn't want to have to put her in danger by disclosing her identity. Ms. Kupper revealed that she was a family friend of one of the parties involved in the Burger King robbery, Santiago Ramirez, and that she knew the details of what had happened.

NYPD detective Michael O'Connor arrived at the 47th Precinct at eight a.m. on Sunday, April 12. Detective O'Connor, a sixteen-year veteran of the force with eleven years as a detective, was assigned to lead the task force of more than fifty detectives and officers investigating the death of Karen Marsh. Detective O'Connor was informed by Sergeant Axberg, a supervisor working the midnight-to-eight-a.m. shift, that a confidential informant had identified a suspect in the case. This was the first time Detective O'Connor knew anything whatsoever about Santiago Ramirez.

By ten a.m., Detective O'Connor, his partner, Detective Sheehy, Sergeant Axberg, and several other detectives had knocked on the door of 2446 University Avenue in the Bronx, looking for Santiago Ramirez. As a precaution, they posted one detective outside the building and others at the back and on the roof. O'Connor took the front door. He put his hand into his coat pocket, then slipped it through a hole he had made in the lining for the purpose of retrieving his revolver from the holster undetected. He kept his weapon drawn and concealed in his coat pocket. He knocked on the door. An eighteen-year-old girl still wearing her nightclothes, Josephine Ramirez, also known as Josie, answered the door. She was nervous. She said Santiago was her brother. She told the detective he wasn't home. Surreptitiously, O'Connor returned his firearm to the holster through the hole in his pocket and entered the apartment. Concerned that family members might alert the suspect the police were looking for him, Detective O'Connor asked Josie and her aunt and uncle, who were also in the apartment, to go with the officers to the precinct to answer questions.

Detectives O'Connor and Sheehy interviewed Josie and explained that the police already knew what had happened and who had done the crime at the Burger King. He said it would be in Josie's best interest if she told them whatever details she knew about it. Josie burst into tears. She became hysterical and began to sob uncontrollably. Detective O'Connor put his arm around her. Josie cried on his shoulder and said over and over that it had been an accident, her brother had told her it was an accident. Detective O'Connor told her not to worry, he would take care of everything, she had no reason to be afraid. After an hour, Josie stopped crying and told the detectives everything she knew. Detective O'Connor asked where her brother was and Josie told them: at their grandparents' house in Anaheim, California.

A picture of the suspect was brought to the precinct. Between two and five p.m., a witness who had been present at the Burger King during the homicide of Karen Marsh was shown what's known as a photo array—that is, six pictures of possible suspects in the case—and identified the picture of Santiago Ramirez as that of the shooter.

At five thirty p.m. on Sunday, April 12, 1981, Detective O'Connor went to the Bronx Criminal Court and obtained an arrest warrant for Santiago Ramirez. Detective O'Connor drove the arrest warrant to the FBI office in New Rochelle, New York, where FBI Special Agent Joe Higgins prepared the necessary documents to obtain a warrant for flight to avoid prosecution.

Four hours later, at six thirty Pacific standard time, Special Agent Charles Sullivan of the FBI's Santa Ana, California, office was off duty, working in his yard when he got the call to come in to work. Sullivan changed his clothes, then went to meet Special Agents James J. Mahoney, William Wright, and Carlos Molina to execute a federal arrest warrant on a man wanted for murder in New York, one Santiago Ramirez.

They drove their own vehicles and met around nine fifteen in the evening at an apartment building at 2119 West Ball Road in Anaheim, California. There were four modest, one-story apartments in several buildings, each with its own numerical address. After speaking with the apartment manager, the four FBI special agents devised a plan for how to approach apartment C, where the suspect was believed to be hiding out. Mahoney would cover the rear door of the apartment while Molina, Wright, and Sullivan would enter by the front. They drew their .38-caliber revolvers and held them ready, pointing at the ground. Molina carried a 12-gauge Remington 870 model shotgun with a three-foot barrel pointed at the sky. They could see a low-light table lamp on inside the apartment, but that was it.

Guns in hand, Agent Wright knocked on the door. An older woman in a bathrobe answered: Grace Topher, the suspect's grandmother. The agent told her they were with the FBI and asked if Santiago Ramirez was in the apartment.

"He's asleep, in the back room," she said.

The agents told her they had a warrant for Santiago's arrest for unlawful flight from New York for murder. They were going to arrest him. As Mahoney stood ready at the back of the apartment outside, Sullivan, Wright, and Molina made their way to the bedroom. The door was open. The room was dark. Wright reached around the doorjamb, flipped on the light, and there he was.

Santiago Joseph Ramirez. Male. Hispanic. Light-skinned. Black hair. Five foot five and 150 pounds. He had a distinguishing feature: a space between his front teeth. He was lying on his back in the bed—head on a pillow, arms outside a white sheet with his hands crossed on his chest. His eyes were open. He looked at the agents. His grandfather was lying in the bed next to him. Sullivan knelt down next to Santiago and said, "You're under arrest for unlawful flight from New York for murder. We're from the FBI."

Santiago didn't move. He said, "It was an accident. I didn't mean to shoot her." To the agents, Santiago didn't appear to be visibly upset. He wasn't crying. He wasn't hysterical. He spoke in a normal tone of voice. The agents ordered Santiago to "get out of the bed." Santiago got up; he was wearing underwear—undershorts and a T-shirt. The agents handcuffed Santiago with his hands behind his back. When they brought him out into the living room, his grandmother asked him, "Why did you do it?"

Santiago said, "It was an accident, Grandma. It was an accident." After hearing that, the FBI agents thought they had better read him his rights. They handed Santiago a copy of the Miranda warning. He put on a pair of glasses to read them. Then the agents took Santiago into custody.

April 4, 1981

Josie Ramirez woke up and found her brother, Santiago, in the living room. He was crying. He pointed to an article in the *Daily News* about a robbery at a Burger King restaurant and said he was involved. His friends Luis and Frankie had been with him. Santiago kept saying it was an accident. Josie left the apartment and came back with her brother's girlfriend, Miriam Torres, who stayed in the apartment with Santiago for the rest of the day. Josie went out to a dance that night and didn't come home. She stayed over at a friend's house. When she returned to the apartment on Sunday, April 5, her brother was gone. Her mother told Josie there was a shotgun in the trunk of her brother Santiago's car. Josie got the shotgun from the car and brought it into the apartment and kept it there overnight. On April 6, Frankie was supposed to pick up the shotgun, but he didn't show up. Josie spoke to Frankie on the phone and told him she was going to throw the shotgun away. Frankie said it wasn't hers to throw away, it belonged to Luis. Josie gave the shotgun to Frankie and he gave it back to Luis on the seventh or eighth of April. Frankie spoke to Josie one more time to let her know that "everything was all right."

FOUR AND A HALF hours after the robbery, from 3:57 a.m. to 4:15 a.m., the Bronx District Attorney's office made a video of the crime scene.

The video begins by first following the path of gunman Frankie Alemar as he enters the Burger King and vaults over the counter. The shooter, or holder of the shotgun, did not go in that direction. The video shows his path, moving along the tables and through a door into the kitchen, where he would have encountered several employees and ordered them to lie down on the floor. The video then moves through the now empty kitchen area to the spot where Karen Marsh was standing, then shows "where in fact Karen Marsh died, and then depicts in rather gory detail her deceased body," according to the defense attorney attempting to keep it from being entered into evidence. The tape then pans back and forth among various patches of blood on the walls and around the room where the shooter had stood over some seven-odd people lying on the floor. The video then goes to the manager's office, in disarray, where Frankie Alemar had demanded money. After receiving the money and hearing the shotgun blast, Alemar left the manager's office. The video follows his path out of the manager's office and into the kitchen, where it ends on the dead body of Karen Marsh.

In the pretrial hearing motions, the defense contended that the video's sole purpose was to inflame the hearts and minds of the jury; that the repeated pans of the scene could have no other purpose but to present and reinforce in the mind of whoever would view this the horror and shocking result of this particular incident.

The defense attorney was right—I wasn't even watching the video, but just the idea of it inflamed my passion. I couldn't stop thinking about it. That video was somewhere in an evidence box in the archives of the police department or the district attorney's office. I could have tracked it down. From writing for *Law & Order*, I had contacts throughout the criminal justice system in New York who could have helped me locate those materials. Hungry for details, I wanted to reconstruct what had happened from every angle and perspective on record. I hoped more information would douse the fire of my curiosity, not feed it. The aftermath didn't end with the crime scene, the arrest, or even the conviction. For me, the aftermath was ongoing.

I wondered how it had been for the rest of my family. My father, in particular, who supervised parolees who were robbers and killers. I thought about how he had burst into tears when he heard the news, then seemed lost and conflicted once we learned it had been an accident. It would stand to reason that the trauma of Karen's murder might have affected the way he dealt with his parolees. But I knew it was the other way around.

I don't remember when. I don't remember where. And I don't remember why. But I remember that sometime before my father died, in 2005, he told me he had gone to a parole hearing for one of Karen's killers. He said he'd told the parole board words to the effect of "This boy destroyed my family. But it was a mistake. He's a young man, and he can still make something of his life. We should let him out."

This sublime act of forgiveness was a stunning request: the hard-boiled parole officer advocating for a convicted killer. The fact that it was my father took my breath away. It was proof that everyone has the capacity for change or, at the very least, a change of heart. While unexpected in some ways, this turn in my father exemplified the complexities and contradictions of his personality. He was controlling yet protective, and sometimes someone to be protected from. Unpredictable.

I wished I could have talked to him to find out what he was thinking. I wanted to understand how he had arrived at the conclusion that he needed to forgive someone he had once plotted to kill. The passage of time could have worn down the jagged edges of his trauma. Or maybe the last thirty years on the job as a parole officer had influenced his decision to lobby for the killer's release. I realized my father must have gone to some trouble—pulling strings and calling in favors—to be allowed to have his say at the hearing. This memory complicated things regarding my decision to write a letter to the parole board about Santiago Ramirez. I didn't doubt that my father had done this, but I wanted something or someone to corroborate this recollection so I could figure out my own course of action.

CHAPTER SEVENTEEN

I went back to Queens for the Thanksgiving holiday. My mother still lived in the house where I was born and raised. I loved being home. The warm, familiar feeling of my old room. The place where I had been forged, that knew me best, that held my memories, but no longer, thankfully, held me.

I unpacked the clothes in my suitcase into the same dresser drawers I'd had since elementary school. I slept in the bottom half of my old bunk bed on a decades-old mattress that shouldn't have been comfortable but still was. The top bunk had been moved across the hall into my sister's room, where ten years earlier my father had died while on home hospice with lung cancer that had spread to his blood, bones, and brain. After that, my mother and I started a new tradition of lying awake under the covers in our own beds and talking into the wee hours of the night across the darkened hallway.

That Thanksgiving eve, in the late-night stillness, we talked about Karen's murder. I asked her if my father had attended any of the parole hearings. Even though he'd never said anything about it to her, my mother remembered that I had told her he'd mentioned it to me. I told her about the pretrial transcript and all the surprising and disturbing things I had learned about the case. She murmured a wounded sigh when I told her that the suspect had reloaded. That Santiago Ramirez had at times laughed during the proceedings. That the defense brought a motion to have Uncle Warren removed and banned from the courtroom. I asked if my father had attended any of the trial. My mother didn't remember.

But she did remember that the mood in our house was tense. She reminded me that Karen's funeral took place on my father's fifty-first birthday. I could almost hear him saying, "Ain't that something. Hell of a way to spend a birthday." He would have been angry that his day was hijacked by a tragedy and he wouldn't be in control or allowed to celebrate the way he wanted. My mother said I was full of piss and vinegar. Snapping at her—which was nothing new. But surprisingly, also talking back to my father. As she recounted this, I felt a twinge, remembering the anger and resentment I'd felt. She said she'd had to force me to sign a birthday card and give him the gift she had wrapped and put my name on for him. I had said he didn't deserve anything. My mother said she understood that I was grieving and struggling to process Karen's murder, but she didn't want my father's feelings to be hurt. She remembered something else. She referred to it as "the incident" with my father. All at once I knew what she was going to say.

A memory I had blocked came flooding back. Of that morning's light streaming through the blinds and laid out like ribbons on the living room floor. My father's bay rum cologne over coffee grinds and cigarette smoke. The ticking of the miniature grandfather clock on the mantel interrupted by the sickening dull thud of bone under skin meeting flesh over bone. A punch, a fall, a struggle. Limbs and bodies scuffled. Images took shape alongside my mother's words.

My father was headed to the Bronx. He made breakfast for himself, left an unscraped plate, eggy skillet, and a white paper towel oiled to a slick yellowed brown by bacon grease on the kitchen counter. My mother pointed to the mess he had left, his dirty dishes not even stacked in the sink, and asked, "Aren't you going to clean that up?"

My father wheeled around and started beating her. I could picture it, though not exactly. He might have punched her or backhanded her across the face or blunted her chin with the heel of his hand. My mother insisted he hit her with an open hand, not a closed fist. I imagined the smack of skin on skin and my mother's startled exhalation of breath when the assault began. I didn't remember if I was nearby: in the foyer, dining room, or kitchenette; or if I had been listening to the confrontation unfold and had run down from upstairs. The details eluded me, hidden in a place where they couldn't hurt me, even as the feeling of rage came roaring back.

My mother said she'd called my name, then cried out, "Come help me!" She said I ran in quick. I remember seeing my father standing over my mother, curled up on the couch.

She said I yelled at my father, "Don't you touch my mother again!" Then I went after him. Pushed him down onto the couch. My mother slipped out from under his fallen body. My palms pulsed with the sense memory of my imperfect blows, how the meat of his muscle gave way to the heel of my hand sinking into his chest and biceps, his shoulder and neck. I punched as hard as I could, but it wasn't hard enough. I didn't draw blood, but I wanted to. I wanted to destroy him, but I couldn't. He curled defensively into a ball—knees up to his forehead, forearms wrapped around his shins. In the shadow under his arm, one black eye looked out at us sideways like a shark.

My mother said we'd yelled at him, "We'll kill you! We will kill you!" Throwing punches and slapping at him until we were out of breath. We stepped back, panting, and watched my father uncoil. Elbows propped up on the couch arm, his feet planted on the ground. My mother said that was the scaredest she had ever seen him. But I remembered a look of stunned disbelief and pained indignation on his face. When he moved to stand, my arms jutted out like daggers to keep my father away. He walked past us and out of the house without saying a word. We didn't talk about what had happened. That was the last time my father ever hit my mother. I pushed it out of my mind and blocked it from my memory.

But as my mother retold the story, I felt an adrenaline rush and an uncomfortable mix of emotions I couldn't identify. This trauma had lived inside me hidden, unexamined, for so long that I didn't know how to process it now. It sat inside my gut like a sack of shards pricking me from the inside. In the bottom bunk of my childhood bed I was afraid of the dark again. I covered myself with pillows and blankets and curled into a ball.

When I got back to Los Angeles, I wanted to remember the incident but couldn't bring myself back to the moment. Instead I remembered a woman at the memorial for my favorite uncle who had passed. She told a story about how Uncle Bill had hypnotized her to stop smoking. I wondered if hypnosis would help me remember the things I had blocked. I found a hypnotherapist in the Valley and called to make an appointment. He was a fast talker with a thick Brooklyn accent. I was oddly reassured to have stumbled on another New Yorker from the outer boroughs, someone I thought would innately understand where I was coming from. But he wouldn't help me. He said helping me remember a memory would be unethical because the power of suggestion was too strong. It's not that he doubted that the incident with my father had happened. He thought I had blocked the event to protect myself from being traumatized. What he felt I needed to understand was why.

He talked quickly as he rattled off several theories having to do with fight or flight, the consciousness of mammals, the lizard brain, and the human propulsion system, which reacts to danger at a cellular level. I wedged my phone between my ear and shoulder, struggled with my free hand to write down on nearby Post-its his insights and theories. He said all I really needed to do was give myself permission to feel it. He said one night before I went to bed I needed to open myself up to remember what had happened and how it had made me feel. That was the only way I could begin to forgive my father for what he had done to my mother, and, more important, to forgive myself for what I had done to my father. The hypnotherapist must have felt my hesitation and said, "You suppressed the memory because it was too painful to acknowledge that you beat your father up." He thought that if I stopped trying to protect myself, my full memory of it would come back to me. I would be free.

I bristled at the thought that I needed to be forgiven for coming to my mother's defense. But I couldn't deny that I had blocked the memory for a reason. I recognized the feeling churning in the pit of my stomach as the warming guilt of shame.

Forgive. Forgive. Forgive.

I didn't know where to begin.

CHAPTER EIGHTEEN

It took more than a year for the Office of Victim Assistance to send me copies of all the parole board hearing transcripts for Karen's killers. During that time, I left the world of teen TV dramas and decided I wanted to go back to writing cop shows. Over the course of my career, I had written for franchises (*Law & Order*, *CSI: Miami*), quirky cop shows (*Homicide: Life on the Street*, *Saving Grace*, *The Glades*), and even a show about parole officers (*Street Time*).

My first job in television was as a script coordinator on a show called *The Cosby Mysteries*. It starred Bill Cosby as a retired NYPD forensic expert and was created by cop drama royalty William Link who, with Richard Levinson, had created *Mannix*, *Columbo*, and *Murder, She Wrote*. The show featured quirky characters by the legendary talent Rita Moreno and a newcomer named Dante Bezé, who went on to become the rapper Mos Def. *The Cosby Mysteries* was being produced during the LAPD investigation of O. J. Simpson for the murders of Nicole Brown Simpson and Ron Goldman. Looking back, I realize how astounding it is to think of how wrong public perception was about those two celebrities, Cosby and OJ. That from a distance it was difficult if not impossible to really know someone based on what you might have heard or read about him.

One of the writers on *The Cosby Mysteries*, the playwright Eric Overmyer, gave me my first writing job in television—an episode of an NBC drama called *Homicide: Life on the Street*, based on the book by David Simon. Eric would become a mentor to me. I was excited when he asked me to join the writing staff on his latest show, *Bosch*. This television series was based on the beloved novels by the bestselling author Michael Connelly about an LAPD detective, Hieronymus Bosch. Bosch was a character I understood and could relate to—a man of few words, a rule breaker who didn't play well with others. He was damaged, forever traumatized by his mother's murder, which had taken place when he was just a kid. He went into law enforcement to get the justice his mother's unsolved murder never did. The series also explored the fraught relationship between the emotionally distant Bosch and Maddie, his teenage daughter.

While I was pondering what to do about Santiago Ramirez, I was given an episode of *Bosch* to write in which one of the main characters was to be shot and injured. In the writers' room we had extensive discussions about the motivation of the suspect who was to carry out the shooting. We needed to figure out who he was and the series of events that led the character to this point in his life. We could make him a crazed sociopath or desperate man. We needed to understand why he would do such a thing.

I was well into a second draft of the script when I started receiving packages from Victim Assistance. Thick manila envelopes stuffed with stacks of documents about Luis Torres and Francisco Alemar arrived at my home. I was still waiting for transcripts from Santiago Ramirez's parole board hearings. I had added my name to the list of people receiving notice of when his hearings would take place. Every now and then I would receive a thin white business envelope in the mail with an official letter notifying me of postponements or his next hearing date. I still hadn't written a letter for or against his release. I still didn't know how I felt.

It bothered me that Luis Torres and Francisco Alemar were already out and living their lives. I couldn't affect their paroles, but I hoped the transcripts would somehow shed more light on Santiago Ramirez, the person he was back then, and clarify if the gun had really gone off accidentally. That was the key to my being able to forgive Ramirez and give him another chance at life. I knew forgiveness was supposed to free me from my anger. But I didn't know if forgiveness was even possible.

I read Alemar's transcripts first. He was more familiar to me. I remembered the photo of him in the newspaper when he surrendered himself to the New York *Daily News*. He was a twenty-year-old technical student studying air-conditioning repair to make a better life for himself. "Look what I have done to my future now," he told the reporter, Daniel O'Grady, after he surrendered. Alemar had taken a plea and was given fifteen years to life. I wondered what he had said or done to convince the parole board that after more than three decades behind bars he should be freed. I braced for unsettling revelations. If the court transcripts had taught me anything, it was that my knowledge of the crime was incomplete and to expect the unexpected. The first surprise was a familiar name at Alemar's initial parole board hearing—Commissioner Gerald Burke.

I had interviewed Commissioner Burke more than a decade earlier for my parole documentary. In the back of my mind I must have known it was a possibility that he could preside over the parole hearings for the boys who killed Karen. Burke was tough but compassionate with a colorful way of speaking and a gallows sense of humor he explained away as a defense mechanism common to people in law enforcement. I heard his voice in my head as I read the commissioner's questions to Alemar in the first parole hearing transcript, from February 20, 1996. "You then entered the Burger King restaurant . . . and then your buddy, Ramirez, decided to blow some little girl's brains out. Why was it necessary for you and your friends to snuff out that young girl's life?"

"It wasn't," Alemar said, then explained he wasn't in the room at the time, that it had been an accident. He described the crime as "terrible" and wished he could take it back. The commissioner scolded him, saying, "Well, you can't. That's a self-serving statement other than maybe you've taken a knife out and slit your own throat."

"I've thought about that," Alemar said.

"Well, you didn't do it, did you?" The commissioner wasn't letting him off the hook.

Alemar replied, "No, I'm a coward."

Alemar's responses seemed honest and raw. Surprisingly unpracticed for a man who had been sitting in prison for the last fifteen years with nothing but time to think of what to say to get himself out, if he was so inclined. But maybe he didn't think he would get out, at least not his first time before the board. Even so, he said he was sorry. "It's something that I'm going to have to just carry with me for the rest of my life . . . I've done it so far." I understood his inability to move past Karen's death—though it made me uncomfortable to think we were both carrying the same burden, both trapped and looking to be freed. I was glad his parole had been denied.

Alemar's second appearance before the parole board was different. More desperate than resigned. I could feel him leaning in. He wanted to get out, and this time he thought he had a chance. He had given thought to what he was going to say, maybe even gotten guidance from other inmates, and was eager to say it. When the commissioners asked why he had gone ahead with the robbery, he said it was a combination of a lot of things, notably peer pressure, immaturity, and machismo.

At twenty years old, Alemar was already a father with a common-law wife. His wife didn't like Santiago Ramirez and had told Alemar not to go with him, begged him not to commit a robbery. But Alemar went because, in his words, "I felt like, she can't tell me what to do." But then he flips and says back then he was more than just macho, immature, and subject to peer pressure. He insists to the parole board that he did good things, too. He had a woman friend with three young children. "I was like a surrogate father to them. I took them milk. That was part of who I was."

The hearing process seemed to encourage this type of flip-flopping. It asked the inmate to take responsibility, then encouraged him to offer excuses for the crimes he had committed. I didn't know how the commissioners would know when he was telling the truth or making more self-serving statements. So when he told a story about his son asking questions about the crime, Alemar said he reminded his son that even though he wasn't the one who'd pulled the trigger, it didn't matter: "I was there, and it's the same thing." It sounded like some kind of twisted humblebrag, designed to absolve him of wrongdoing by subtly reminding the commissioners that he wasn't the one who'd fired the fatal shot. It was hard for me to take what Alemar said at face value. I started to pick his words apart, looking for the deeper motive behind what he'd chosen to reveal. The writer in me studied him like a character I might create. What did the character want or say he wanted? To get out of prison, obviously. But what did he need? The answer was in what he said about his seventeen-year-old son, who asked his father repeatedly about the crime itself. Alemar admitted, "Now that we're getting to talk to each other a lot more, I'm realizing more and more how awful it was what I did." He said he wanted to make himself "not seem so—such a bad guy." He ends by saying he wants to be a good husband and a father. "I'm asking that you please give me a chance to rejoin society. I can prove that I'm a better human being, a worthwhile human being."

Parole was denied.

Alemar would go before the parole board nine times, once every twenty-four months for eighteen years. By all accounts Alemar was a model prisoner. He was "an excellent inmate" with "no disciplines" except for his "one and only ticket . . . back in 1991." He took all the vocational and self-improvement classes he could, including programs in substance abuse, aggression, community prep, and children's advocacy. Alemar was determined to keep busy. "I structure my life to avoid problems. There's a lot of problems you can get into in here, but if you structure your life correctly."

"You keep to yourself?" the commissioner at his eighth appearance asks.

"No, I get out a lot. I help. I do a lot of things, but I structure myself, my life so I stay away from those bad influences."

One of the good influences that Alemar had was his family. I was stunned to learn that while he was in prison Alemar had met his wife on what was essentially a blind date, married a year later, and had children.

"A friend of mine was—his wife came to visit and brought

a friend. And he asked me if I wanted to go to a visit and I went." He said they "got to talking and it snowballed."

"You're smiling," the commissioner notes. "I mean, you're telling the story and you're smiling . . ."

"It's a nice memory," Alemar says. "She visit me for about a year before we got married."

He had four children: one son, three daughters. "Two of them were—we had trailer visits." And three grandchildren. Alemar was a family man.

Despite his circumstances, he'd managed to create a life for himself full of work and loved ones. It was maddening, since Karen had never had that chance. But if I was looking for proof that people could change and improve in prison, there it was.

There was so much about Alemar to recommend him. He said he worked in the prison hospital with AIDS patients. "I've had my hands inside men's wounds when nobody else wanted to work with them. I've had to clean them when they were incontinent, when they couldn't take care of themselves." He claimed to have done these things as "an atonement for what I did." Transcripts showed me a man I didn't expect to see, with revelations I never anticipated, on a journey I didn't think was possible. I was begrudgingly impressed—but also deeply conflicted about my contradictory feelings about the man, ashamed to acknowledge that a part of me didn't want him to succeed. Maybe that's why I second-guessed everything he said. Over nearly two decades, Alemar's answers revealed a man genuinely struggling to understand why he had taken part in the crime in the first place and how he could be better. True, his freedom depended on his answering those questions. But Karen's death seemed to weigh heavily on his mind and in his soul. I realized that honestly looking for answers and making excuses about one's behavior are not mutually exclusive.

At one hearing he offered as an excuse that he had no excuse. At another hearing he blamed his upbringing, what he'd learned growing up. "I realize now I didn't really have a normal childhood, although to me it was normal." His father was a violent alcoholic who beat his mother and abandoned the family when Alemar was five. His stepfather was a drug addict who died in prison. His mother's next boyfriend was a convicted rapist. According to Alemar, all the men his mother dated, his father figures, "they all committed crimes. They never worked. None of them worked. This is what I saw. So I never thought that crime was something that you shouldn't do."

Alemar's answers could have been coached, concocted after therapy sessions with mental health professionals and other inmates telling him what they thought the parole board would want to hear. He said, "I'm sorry for the crime that I committed and for the death of Karen Marsh."

I went back and listened to my recorded interview with Commissioner Burke explaining the parole board hearing. How the inmate starts to parrot back what he learns in whatever therapy group he's in. If the group's leader says to take responsibility, that's what the inmate does. If they say find God, the inmate gets religion. If they say you are a product of your surroundings, the inmate blames his surroundings. Alemar was in a program called Exodus, in which he said he was able to "face my past." Through the process of trying to figure out what to say to the parole board, he found the truth. It wasn't until his ninth appearance that Alemar had a revelation and came clean.

"I lied to myself and I lied to the parole board," Alemar

said. It wasn't peer pressure or bad role models, he explained. "I had other role models, good role models that I didn't—I could have chosen to learn from . . . I realize that all along I wanted to be a man, but what I wanted was to be the kind of man that my mother loved . . . bad guys." Once he realized that, he said things started to fall into place and he understood that he was rationalizing his behavior. He didn't worry about consequences, but now he knew that "everything I say, everything I do, everything has consequences."

He was a long way from the twenty-year-old who ranted about ruining his life. Now he was fifty. As time wore on, and his children, particularly his daughters, grew up and reached Karen's age, he started to understand what he had done. That this was his fault. But it was something he said at the end of his statement that touched me deeply and opened my heart to forgiveness. "Karen Marsh you said would have lived another sixty years. Karen Marsh is still alive inside of me. She's never going to die as long as I'm alive." Alemar said he wanted "to be able to live a life in honor of the memory of Karen Marsh."

I believed him.

Part of the reason I believed him was because, in another surprising turn, he had owned up to the truth. Over the years, the transcripts reveal a gradual, albeit sometimes unwitting, admission that Alemar and his codefendants had committed robbery before.

When Karen was killed, newspaper accounts reported that the Burger King robbery had been the first such crime for Alemar and his codefendants. But that wasn't true. From the presentencing investigation report, the parole commissioners knew, and when questioned, Alemar confirmed, that on

March 20, 1981, the three boys had robbed another fast-food restaurant, a McDonald's on 204th Street and Bainbridge Avenue in the Bronx. "That was the first one," Alemar said, making it seem like the boys had done only two robberies in total. But at a later hearing, when answering a different question about whether or not he was prepared to use the gun he carried into the Burger King, he let slip that because he had done two robberies before, "I knew for myself that nobody was going to get hurt, because we just weren't there to hurt anybody."

By the ninth and what would be his final parole hearing, Alemar was ready and willing to honestly answer the commissioner's question: "Were you robbing numerous locations at that time?"

"Yes, we robbed several places," he said.

"But you just got caught when this occurred?"

"On this one, yeah."

THE WHEELMAN IN THE crime, Luis Torres, never admitted to the other robberies. Unlike Alemar's raw and brutally honest responses to the commissioners' questions, Torres seemed to be lying, or at least conveniently concealing the whole truth. The commissioner called him on it, saying, "Your role looks like it was a little bit more than what you're remembering today." As the wheelman, Torres had some deniability when it came to what happened inside the Burger King. The truth was, Torres wasn't there when Karen was killed.

During the robbery, Torres sat in the car, parked a block away from the Burger King. Far enough away that he couldn't see the restaurant or hear the shotgun blast that took Karen's life. The first Torres knew about anybody getting hurt was when Ramirez rushed back to the car, carrying the shotgun. Then Alemar jumped into the back seat, with a wad of cash and a .38-caliber handgun. Torres said they mumbled that the gun went off and that it was an accident, but they didn't specify exactly what the accident was. They went back to Alemar's house, where they divided up the money—which, according to the parole hearing transcripts, was $1,651, much more than the $241 quoted in the newspaper. At Alemar's home they turned on the news, and that's when Torres said he "realized it went wrong."

During that first parole hearing, Torres didn't think to apologize for Karen's death until the commissioner asked him, "You're sorry that happened, right?" Torres replied matter-of-factly, "Yes, I am." And left it at that. He never used the word "sorry"; instead, he said he "deeply apologized." He made a perfunctory statement that included all the clichéd phrases about the pain he had caused the family and how he wanted to turn back the hands of time, without demonstrating any of the actual depth of feeling those phrases were meant to convey. The parole board continued to deny his parole, stating in its official decisions that the denial was due to Torres's "lack of remorse and minimization of [his] actions." The board decided that his release was "incompatible with the welfare and safety of the community." He was deemed "a serious risk" because "the crime represents a propensity for extreme violence."

Despite all this, the hearing transcripts reveal the commissioners were conflicted about Torres. He was a model prisoner. Even better than Alemar. He had a long list of achievements. Torres had earned a GED, a BS from Marist College, a paralegal certificate, and a bilingual studies certificate. He also learned vocational trades like welding, carpentry, plumbing, and machine repair. At one point he was the prison's auto mechanic, responsible for maintaining all eighty-seven vehicles at the facility. Because he had a clean disciplinary record in 1992, he earned an outside pass and was assigned the job of driving the prison bus and taxi. Every time Torres came before the board, he had learned something new or earned a new certificate.

At his seventh parole board hearing, the commissioner said, "I'll be honest with you, Mr. Torres, on paper this is probably one of the most difficult cases I have seen. . . . You have commendations and certificates and things that you don't see everyday. So clearly you've done a lot of work on yourself and it shows potential growth and development over the years." That was the problem for me. Taking classes, earning certificates, and improving his chances for employment on the outside didn't mean he had changed. I still blamed Torres for what happened to Karen. Torres supplied the guns, a sawed-off shotgun and a .38-caliber pistol. Then he lied about it to the parole board.

Sounding impatient and full of attitude, Torres first said he'd found the shotgun in his backyard and sawed off the ends himself. He insisted he kept the shotgun for his own protection. "The neighborhood I come from, it's a rough neighborhood." He explained this with no self-awareness whatsoever that he might have been responsible for that condition. He denied an earlier statement in his presentencing report that he had rented the .38 from a friend. Now he said he guessed Alemar had the .38 at the time. There were many discrepancies between what he had said for the official record after he was convicted and what he was saying decades afterward to the parole board. It wasn't until a later parole hearing that

Torres came clean about where the guns had come from: he'd stolen them. Before he helped rob the Burger King, Torres on his own had burglarized a house. He told the commissioners, "I obtained the firearm and the shotgun during a previous burglary."

I was not impressed by this unexpected although not altogether surprising confession. I needed Torres to be full of remorse, especially after Alemar's unexpected impressive transformation and dedication to being better for Karen. It seemed to me that Alemar was genuinely trying to figure things out, while Torres just wanted to prove that he had changed. Even if he really hadn't.

In order to forgive Torres—and therefore, down the road, Ramirez—I needed proof that he was sorry. Not just because he had been in prison for thirty years, but because Karen had lost her life. My forgiveness was conditional and had limits. It didn't feel like true forgiveness. What was forgiveness, anyway? I tried to remember what had been said about it from people like Gandhi, Martin Luther King Jr., and Nelson Mandela. The platitudes about only light driving out darkness and forgiveness liberating the soul, its being an attribute of the strong, didn't help my particular situation. Even though I was an atheist now, forgiveness had been an essential part of my Christian upbringing—the idea of loving your enemies and turning the other cheek chief among the beliefs I had been taught to follow in elementary school. But I knew from my high school peers that in the Jewish faith, forgiveness was conditional on *teshuva*—repentance. Torres had not done that. Although I subscribed to the saying that we should forgive people for what they do, not who they are, I was angry at Torres for what he had done.

Letting go of my anger at Torres meant sympathizing with him, somehow putting myself in his shoes. Again, I tried to think of Torres as a character I was writing and what that character would be feeling. I could see how that character's blame could be mitigated—he had been in the car. Torres didn't see Karen. He never saw her alive. He never saw her with her face blown off. I could understand that he probably didn't think it was his fault. I could imagine the fear and panic he must have felt, thinking his life was over. I felt it rising in my own throat. The sense of being suffocated. Losing one's freedom. Making a mistake that could not be corrected—at least not immediately, but maybe over time he could prove that this one mistake did not define who he was. Maybe he did think that by taking every opportunity, every course the prison had to offer, he could prove he was worthy and deserved to be freed. Maybe that was his way of making amends. But it wasn't enough. It would never be enough. No amount of classes or certificates could ever make up for taking a life. How could it? What could he possibly do to make that right?

Then something happened.

By 2006 Torres had been granted privileges to work outside the prison. He drove a van. He left the site. He had so many skills he was asked to work in construction. One day while in the field he heard a commotion, then saw a man buried alive. Without a second thought for his own safety, he rushed to help. Using only his bare hands, he dug the man out. He saved a man's life.

By his seventh parole hearing, the story was well known. Still, the commissioners wanted him to tell it. It's thrilling. The prisoner who took a life saved a life. The man Torres saved wrote letters on his behalf. Everyone was rooting for Torres to get out—except for the family of the girl he had killed. It made me feel petty. Incapable of compassion. The well of my sorrow was too deep to climb out of, even if it was filled with his good deeds. But my forgiveness didn't matter. Torres had finally, accidentally, found a way to prove that he was worthy of a second chance. After his eighth appearance before the parole board, Torres's parole was granted. Even I have to admit it's a good story. A life for a life. I couldn't have written it any better.

Torres is out. There's nothing I can do but accept it. This is not a feeling of forgiveness so much as resignation. And I was still no closer to understanding how to forgive Santiago Ramirez. His next parole hearing date was less than a year away.

CHAPTER NINETEEN

Santiago Ramirez was taken into custody by the FBI on Sunday, April 12, 1981. He stayed in detention until April 27, then was flown back to New York, where he was picked out of a lineup by witnesses from the Burger King who identified him as the shooter. The second gunman and the wheelman turned themselves in to the *Daily News* and the NYPD in the Bronx on April 13. I don't remember how I found out Karen's killers had been arrested, if my mother told me or I read it in the newspaper. I do remember being relieved that the anguish of knowing Karen's killers was out there, walking free, was over. There would be justice for Karen.

This reprieve was temporary. Relief quickly gave way to depression. At least when the police were looking for the killers, I had something to hope for, a definable end to this trauma: capture, arrest, conviction. Now all I was left with was unending grief and no idea how to quell the mourning pain. Once the killers were in custody, the dead girl, the murdered daughter of a homicide detective, was out of the news. The story was over. My parents and I didn't talk about Karen or discuss the murder anymore. Outwardly, everyone acted as though it was time to move on—except I wasn't ready. I felt like I had been pulled down through the floor into a bottomless sorrow.

My father resumed his regular weekend visits to see his mother in the Bronx. I went with him at first. Riding in the car, just the two of us, he listened to the radio, I looked out the window. We never spoke about what had happened between us, him beating my mother and my coming to her defense by beating him back. I had already blocked the incident, my mind protecting me from another trauma. Aunt Barbara was protecting herself, too. She called my mother and asked that I not come around anymore. Seeing me was a too-painful reminder of the daughter she had lost. I stopped going to the Bronx.

I stopped doing homework. I stopped caring about getting good grades and pleasing my parents. I stopped worrying about whether or not I was liked or had friends. After classes, I left school quickly and retreated to the sanctuary of my room.

I'd lost my bearings, but I knew one thing: I wanted to be free. I wanted to get away from my father's rules, my mother's expectations. Ironically, that meant I had to do what was expected of me and follow the rules so that I could get into a good college and move away. With senior year approaching, this was my last chance to participate in activities that would look good on my college applications and prove I deserved to be admitted. It was like trying to get parole—taking classes, earning certificates, doing activities, to show I was worthy of freedom.

The SATs were my first hurdle. Less than a month away, I was resigned to not doing well my first time out. I knew that a few months later I would have another chance to take the test. I was focused on the summer and my plans to work as an intern at the Cloisters museum.

The Cloisters was part of the medieval collection of the Metropolitan Museum of Art. Except the Cloisters wasn't anywhere near the Met. The Cloisters' art collection was housed in a sprawling medieval-looking compound that resembled a

European monastery on top of a hill and was so far uptown in Manhattan it was almost in the Bronx. The building's design featured four cloisters—hence the museum's name—that had been purchased from several French abbeys, convents, and monasteries and rebuilt stone by stone inside the museum. The Cloisters was magical. But it was in a troubled neighborhood. I was worried my parents would change their minds about letting me go. But they agreed this internship would look good on my college applications. They signed the permission form and extracted a promise from me that I would never take the dangerous, even if faster, A train to get there.

That summer, my daily commute on the M4 bus took two and a half hours each way. I always sat in the first forward-facing seat, next to the window on the right-hand side of the bus, closest to the sidewalk. I wanted a better look at the shifting landscape of Madison Avenue. I watched the white Upper East Side of Manhattan, with its storefront art galleries, red-brick buildings, brownstones, and doormen in blue uniforms with gold braiding standing outside apartments morph into the dilapidated tenements with gargoyles propping up windows, sitting atop fake columns, in Spanish and Black Harlem.

The bus terminated outside the grand stone entrance of Fort Tryon Park. There was a pay phone to call the museum and request the employee van that shuttled us workers through the beautiful albeit crime- and rodent-infested woods, so overgrown and leafy green that summer, and full of hidden dangers.

The design of the Cloisters was patterned after a Benedictine monastery, which, instead of highlighting the isolation of individuals, used architecture to emphasize the sense of community. I loved being there. I left home in the early-morning dark and returned in the late light of summer nights. The building overlooked the Hudson River and had a panoramic view of the tree-lined New Jersey Palisades on the other side. The religious imagery of the medieval art was comfortingly familiar. The annunciation, the virgin birth, the resurrection. I didn't believe in those stories anymore. The blind faith of my childhood was gone. I appreciated the stories from a distance, though, as salves meant to lessen and distract from the traumas that befell medieval life, the horrors of illness, the randomness of death.

I gave tours to awed tourists from abroad, bored teenagers from expensive summer camps on Long Island, and boisterous church groups from the outer boroughs. I designed all my tours to end with the Unicorn Tapestries—seven insanely beautiful wall-size tapestries woven in the early sixteenth century that told the story of a unicorn hunt, an allegory for either Christ's resurrection or the hunt for love. I spent hours in the room where they hung, studying the details in the figures, finding the intricately woven flora and fauna in the background. I was drawn to the sixth tapestry, in which the unicorn is viciously slain by hunters, stabbed in the throat and flank, with another hunter's sword poised to pierce its neck. The unicorn is tossed limp-necked over the back of a horse and carried off, only to be miraculously resurrected in the seventh, final tapestry. Blood still dripping from its wounds, the unicorn sits regally in a field of flowers, enclosed by a wooden fence, chained to a tree by a golden tether. A pretty prison. Caged but still alive, patiently waiting to be freed.

When my shift in the galleries was over, I would disappear through one of the many secret passageways that led to the hidden employee-only spaces. I spent hours in the upstairs library researching or down in the workshop learning medieval crafts—calligraphy, tapestry weaving, gilt painting, stained-glass window making. It was a job, but it felt like freedom. For the first time ever, I was sad to see the summer end.

Senior year I focused on getting into college. I stayed away from classes that would pull my grade point average down, like calculus and organic chemistry, and substituted drama and Latin. Now instead of being on my high school's science core track with the hardcore nerds, I was taking classes in humanities, surrounded by theater and art geeks. That put me out of sync with the classmates I had been with for three years, including Lisa. We saw each other in the hallway and exchanged pleasantries about our parents, the SATs, and her new boyfriend like nothing had changed. And between us, it hadn't. Our friendship was the same. I was different.

How much I had changed became clear when I was asked to give a speech at a school assembly for Arista, my high school's branch of the New York public school system's honor society. I faced an auditorium full of students, teachers, and parents and quoted Shakespeare, to thine own self be true, and advised my peers not to worry about what everybody else wanted for them. "Follow your purpose," I said. My purpose was just to be me, whatever that entailed. There was no right or wrong. And if your purpose was to take a life, my purpose was to stop you. There was no obligation to your race, your gender, your school, or your parents.

People asked if I had written the speech all by myself. I was able to laugh off the backhanded compliment because I had support. I had made friends. Best friends. Three girls I never would have met in the science classes I used to take. Cathy was proud Queens-born Irish with long, straight black hair down her back and unrequited crushes on boys that fueled her poetry. After school we went to Gaby's Pizza for a slice, played *Ms. Pac-Man* in the arcade, then hung out for hours at her house on the other side of the Long Island Rail Road tracks. Judy was Black and Jewish, soft-spoken with a powerful singing voice. She took me to my first *Messiah* sing that Christmas, and invited me to sleepovers at her house, where I met her older brother, a trumpet player at the Queens College school of music, who became my first boyfriend. Dominique was second-generation Haitian, unapologetic and brutally honest. She liked to keep her own company and showed me it was okay to do the same. In my senior yearbook, she wrote that I was one of the few people with whom she felt comfortable enough to show "the real me. I'm not really as cool and tough as I pretend and I think you realize that. But with you I don't worry about that. I think we can even sit around together and not say anything. Sometimes I really wish we were related." With these girls I had the kind of friendship I'd convinced myself I would have had with Karen. Close, connected, with real understanding, and effortless. But looking back on my teenage relationship with Karen, I can see that something about it just didn't add up. On the surface we had so much in common, and I wanted that to be true. But if I was being honest, I had to admit that Karen and I never would have been friends.

I could count on one hand the times Karen and I had done things together: her Sweet Sixteen and mine; her sleepover, then mine. There were photographs of all us kids in the basement of my house. Mugging for the camera in shirt sleeves, tank tops, and shorts—the summer. There was my memory of another visit sitting cross-legged in my closet when Karen taught me how to kiss a boy by practicing on a pillow. Only two months older than me, she was worldly-wise. There was a spring weekend when heavy winds whipped across the Triborough Bridge and Aunt Barbara said they couldn't make the trip out to Queens in her VW bug. I watched the weather, hoping it would change. My disappointment was bitter and profound. Life felt unfair, and I was inconsolable when the day passed and I didn't get to see Karen.

Usually I saw Karen when I went with my father to see his mother in the Bronx. Karen was the reason I went in the first place. After sitting with Grandma, we would amble up the block to visit the rest of the family. We came together in Aunt Barbara's living room or squeezed around the small kitchen table having cold drinks in the summer, hot in the winter. We sat with our parents. An official state visit of sorts. Subdued, smiling, sometimes laughing knowingly at the ridiculousness of adults. We waited patiently to interject the appropriate anecdotes about what was going on in our lives—report cards with all As, awards for extracurricular activities, an acknowledgment in the local newspaper or church newsletter for myriad other accomplishments. The things parents cared about. Never anything bad, unfortunate, or unhappy. Never anything about how we felt, just how we were doing in our respective worlds. We never ventured off on our own to play when we were kids or as we got older to gossip and reveal our secrets—hopes, dreams, and fears—as I imagined we would have. When I did go up to Karen's room it was to see a new piece of furniture, a new item of clothing. Sometimes she'd excuse herself and leave to get back to homework, chores, or whatever weekend plans she had. And I wished I could go with her. But most of the time when I went to the Bronx with my father, Karen wasn't home.

I was afraid that I was the cousin Karen was forced to see. The relative she had to invite to her sleepover because her parents made her. The same way she had to invite me to her sweet sixteen. The reason she came late to mine, because she didn't really want to be there. Maybe every time I went to visit Grandma, Karen made herself scarce on purpose. I winced, stung by the realization that I didn't know what Karen really thought about me. She was always friendly, but I wasn't sure she was really my friend. Or that I was hers.

I could have called Karen more on the phone, made my parents take me to see her more often. But I didn't. Maybe I liked the idea of us being friends more than I wanted us to be friends. Maybe I didn't know how to be friends. Or maybe what I wanted from Karen was acceptance and approval of who I was. Then maybe I could have been free to be myself.

CHAPTER TWENTY

When I was sixteen, my sixteen-year-old cousin, Karen Marsh, had her face blown off by a sawed-off shotgun in a robbery gone awry at a local Burger King in the Bronx. Her brother Warren Marsh asked me to write a letter against granting parole for Karen's killer, Santiago Ramirez.

After Karen was killed I decided there was no God. I was in charge of my life, my destiny. I was in control. I was God. Except for one thing.

Everyone dies. Everyone. Including sometimes beautiful and smart sixteen-year-old girls with their whole lives ahead of them. Maybe Karen died sooner than she should have. But maybe she would have walked out of that Burger King and been run over by a bus. Maybe she would have found out that she had cancer and died anyway. And then who would we blame? Not Santiago Ramirez, the man who pulled the trigger.

He said it was an accident. He'd never handled a sawed-off shotgun before. He didn't mean to kill her. But he fled to California because he knew the only thing worse than killing a cop was killing a cop's child—which Karen was. Her father was a decorated homicide detective. My father was a parole officer. And Santiago Ramirez was right. If the *Daily News* had not printed his side of the story and if the FBI had not brought him back safely, my uncle and my father would have found him and killed him. More death, more dying, more families ruined. More pain. But not for Karen.

Karen died instantly. Shot at point-blank range. With one blast, it was over. The rest of us are the ones who are in pain. And now that Santiago Ramirez is up for parole, thirty-three years later, it's like we are a bloody open wound all over again.

We aren't asking the parole board to punish Santiago Ramirez for Karen; we're asking the parole board to punish him for us. For the pain we continue to live with every day. Because for the family, it's not over. Memories of Karen surface on her birthday and mine. Then again on the day she was killed, on the day she was buried, on the day Santiago Ramirez was caught, and on the day he went to trial. And now there will be a new day—the day Santiago goes before the parole board. I'll be forced to remember this new day until his application for parole is accepted or if rejected for the rest of his life—or ours, whichever ends first. Because death is the only way this pain ends. Unless we can somehow figure out how to forgive.

I once heard it said that forgiveness is being able to accept that you can't change the outcome. I've heard people say, "Don't put a question mark where God has put a period." But I am God, so I should be able to stop this, to forgive—if for no other reason than not forgiving hurts only me.

I don't know how to forgive Santiago Ramirez. But I know it's not going to happen as long as I exercise my power to keep him locked up. As long as he is inside, I am invested in his worthlessness. In the idea that he was a bad person who took a good life. He'll never be able to replace Karen's life. He'll never accomplish what we would like to believe Karen would have or could have done. But we should make him try.

He owes us a good life. A life as good as the one Karen would have lived. A life spent trying. Working hard. Being better. I say let Santiago Ramirez out and let him live up to that. Let him out and let's see if I can start to forgive. Because it truly is madness to continue this way with no end in sight.

I know this is not the letter my cousin Warren expected me to write. But we know from Karen's death that life is full of the unexpected. And learning to deal with the unexpected is what life is about. Karen never had that chance. We do. I submit this letter to the parole board so that Mr. Ramirez, my cousin Warren, and I can finally be set free.

CHAPTER TWENTY-ONE

The copied pages of the transcript were littered with thick black marks. Slashes of permanent marker covered names, job titles, and any identifying nouns or adjectives of everyone except the guilty parties—Ramirez and his codefendants. Curiously, even Karen's name was blacked out. Meant to conceal and protect, these black marks had the opposite effect, and made me think even more about who was being redacted from the story.

By the time I received all the parole hearing transcripts for Santiago Ramirez, he had been in prison for thirty-three years. "I'm kind of nervous," Ramirez said during the early parole hearings. In the transcripts his words faltered, his speech was halting. The commissioners were solicitous and reminded him to take his time. But he couldn't, saying, "This is a very important moment in my life."

Ramirez was doing everything he could to earn parole. He had completed every program the Department of Corrections asked him to complete. He said, "I'm always trying to become a better person every day, you know. And I have to be empowered with different skills and different information to do so." He completed aggression replacement training and worked with the Youth Assistance Program (YAP), for which he wrote a training manual called *Breaking the Cycle and the Chains.* He had held numerous jobs with titles so broad and vague I could only guess at what they entailed: utility gang, laundry operator, gymnasium porter, maintenance laborer, industry worker, typist, clerk, teacher's aide, lawn and grounds.

At one hearing, he explained his work ethic. "Sometime ago, I read a saying in a classroom, 'The descent to hell is easy, the gates are open day and night, but to reclimb that slope and reach the upper end, there is labor.'" He said every job he had felt like "I'm climbing that slope. I know I have a ways to go and a lot of hard work ahead of me." He found his true calling in asbestos removal. Removing asbestos was something he really enjoyed. He said, "It allows me to really give back . . . knowing that I'm doing the right thing and that I'm going to help other people not become exposed to asbestos . . . I take pride in trying to protect life and preserve life." This sounded ridiculous to me. He was either delusional or desperate to appear as though he had changed. He wanted to be free, and asbestos removal had earned him the privilege of working outside the prison walls. He'd had a little taste of freedom and was determined to get out for good.

Even though his own appeals were over, he worked at the law library. He had jobs as a paralegal, a law clerk, and a legal research course instructor, helping other inmates. To the parole board, he said these jobs helped him to realize "that I have to follow the rules and regulations, because I'm an example. I'm going to need that attitude upon my release to respect the laws and the rules and regulation of society."

He was also concerned with the rules and regulations of religion. "I rekindled my relationship with God." Besides working for the chaplain, he had completed the New York Theological Seminary Certificate Program. Karen's murder had made both of us change our mind about God. I lost my faith and he found his, keeping the balance sheet of believers and non- even on both sides. That seemed to be even more proof that religion was man-made, a salve to ease whatever pain we were experiencing. Religion had helped Ramirez clean up his act in a quest for freedom. He said God had "given me the strength to become the man that I am." The man that he had been was troubled.

Ramirez had "received numerous disciplinary tickets for various violations of institutional rules," including an assault on staff, violating direct orders, and possessing contraband and drugs. One commissioner described Ramirez as a "vicious killer" and said, "Based on your disciplinary history and despite your lengthy incarceration, you have failed to conform your behavior as a civil and potentially law-abiding person otherwise would." That's because Ramirez was a drug addict.

Ramirez started using drugs in 1976, when he was fifteen years old. He told the commissioners he started out with marijuana and alcohol, then progressed to LSD, mescaline, cocaine, and finally heroin. He said he turned to drugs because he liked the way they made him feel. He also liked the lifestyle that went along with drugs and "the attention I was getting from the street." After barely graduating from high school, he worked at a print shop, where he did drugs on the job, "which is very dangerous because I'm around machinery, equipment that can rip your hand right off your body. Dangerous for the other people that I'm around."

He admitted that "in fact, I didn't stop using drugs until fourteen years into the sentence, which was 1995." He got clean in December of that year and credited the judge in his case. "This may sound strange, for the sentence he gave me. Because had he given me anything less, it would have did me no good. I still would have continued to use drugs." He said he had a total disregard for the law and lack of self-respect due to feelings of abandonment. For this he blamed his family situation.

In a familiar prisoner refrain, he said that although "I had my mother, I never had that male figure." At early parole hearings, he said, "My father returned from Vietnam addicted to heroin. My uncle committed suicide while in prison, and my grandfather moved away." It reminded me of the mantra I used to express how Karen had been killed. But over the years, Ramirez changed his phrasing. The sentence structure was improved to include how the events had affected him. So in later hearings, he said, "My father returned from the Vietnam War addicted to heroin. I felt alone. My grandfather moved to another state. I felt abandoned. My uncle committed suicide in prison, and I felt betrayed." Even if what he said was true, it felt like he had been coached. I doubted this enlightenment had changed him. Was he speaking his truth or merely telling the parole board what he was told they wanted to hear?

It came as no surprise to learn that Ramirez had been high when he committed the robbery. "On that particular day, there at work, I began my lunch break taking a tab of acid, smoking a joint, and having a beer. After work I continued to smoke weed, and I continued to drink a couple of beers, and that was the events leading up to the robbery." Over the course of nine parole hearings and eight postponements spanning thirteen years he revealed the details of exactly what happened and why.

It all started with a traffic ticket.

Ramirez was caught driving without car insurance. He went to court, where the judge imposed a $500 fine and suspended his license until the fine was paid. Even though he was working, "making a pretty decent buck at the time," he decided to commit a robbery to get the money. Ramirez was the mastermind; he picked the place to rob. The night before the robbery, Ramirez, Alemar, and Torres cased the Burger King restaurant on White Plains Road. They went back the following night around eleven thirty, right before closing. "One of my codefendants was armed with a .32 [*sic*] pistol. I was armed with a loaded sawed-off shotgun." The Burger King restaurant was underneath an elevated train station. The three men lay in wait. They stood off to the side, watching to see when they could go in. An employee showed up late, and when another employee inside opened the front door for her, they went in as well.

On the other side of the restaurant was the kitchen, the manager's office, and an open waiting area before the back exit. Ramirez said he "forcefully told all my victims to proceed to the back of the restaurant," the waiting area. He yelled at them to lie facedown on the ground. The plan was for Ramirez to get to the back exit so that when Alemar, his codefendant with the .38-caliber pistol, got the money from the safe in the manager's office, they could quickly "get out the restaurant and go on our way." Ramirez moved toward the exit. But as he tried to step over the people on the ground, he stepped on somebody's leg. "They moved and I lost my balance and I fired the shotgun."

A commissioner says in a later transcript that there were reports "a tray had fallen and the noise may have caused Ramirez to turn around suddenly." After hearing this, Ramirez amended his account and said, "The trays fell, and I tried to use the trays as leverage to step over the victims. As I stepped onto the tray, I guess my weight might have been too much and one of my victims moved, and I pulled the trigger."

Either way, the shotgun, loaded with buckshot, went off with a loud boom. Ramirez said he was maybe "three feet, four feet, five feet away" from Karen and Desiree Henderson, both lying facedown. No one screamed. Or made a sound. Everybody was quiet. Even Desiree, who was hit by buckshot in the face and neck and suffered permanent hearing damage. Karen was hit in the head and killed instantly.

I felt like the wind had been knocked out of me. I realized this was the most detailed and probably accurate description of the robbery that I had come across. I always thought Karen was standing at the cash register when she was shot, not lying facedown on the floor. What I had envisioned for all these years was not true. Karen had not stared down the barrel of a shotgun. I found solace in the thought that maybe Karen hadn't seen it coming. Maybe she felt no pain. Or very little and certainly not for very long. Maybe she had no idea that she was going to die.

Ramirez was in shock. Too stunned and scared to speak, he was propelled toward the exit as the shotgun went off. He yelled at his codefendant, "Let's go!" He waited "a couple of seconds . . . three or four seconds." But when Alemar didn't come out of the manager's office or respond, Ramirez said, "I just ran out of the store."

Except he didn't.

He left something out of the retelling: he reloaded the shotgun.

"Witnesses who looked up, after the shot, saw Ramirez calmly and methodically empty the gun of the discharged shell and place a new one in it." Only after a commissioner jogged Ramirez's memory with this statement did he concede, "I don't dispute the record." The question was why he reloaded.

Over the years he offered a litany of excuses, including that he had no excuse. He repeatedly said he was shocked, scared, and afraid. Once he said, "I really didn't know what would happen next so I reloaded the gun to maintain control." At another hearing he explained that he had done it "instinctively"—even though he also claimed "I had never fired a shotgun before or a gun." He said he knew how to reload a shotgun only because he had watched it on TV. At a later parole board hearing, he admitted that this idea of reloading the gun "instinctively" had come from working through this issue with someone at the prison.

Over the years, the commissioners dissected every angle of this moment, trying to understand the motives and therefore the man. "I mean, one reloads a weapon because you perceive there is still a danger to yourself or still the need to have a loaded weapon, right?" "If it was an accident and you were so shocked, why didn't you just panic and take flight, at that point, instead of reloading, carrying on with the robbery?"

But carry on they did. Ramirez drove the getaway car back to Alemar's apartment, where they divided the money. Ramirez claims it wasn't until later Saturday morning, when he saw a newspaper, that he realized "I had killed a young lady, injured another." On Sunday he boarded a plane to California.

The commissioners had a hard time believing Ramirez didn't know he had killed Karen. The usually cordial Q&A felt more like an interrogation than an interview. "I mean, but you are literally on top of them, right?" They were incredulous, hostile. "Part of this girl's head was blown off, you didn't even look down to see what happened, as a result of the discharge of the weapon?" Ramirez insisted he didn't see where he had fired, he wasn't looking where the blast went, and he was already headed for the exit and on the other side of the restaurant.

"So you want us to believe that you didn't see the blood and flesh that came off of the victim? Is that what you want us to believe?"

"That's exactly what happened, sir. I didn't see any."

"There is no one screaming as to the gore of what happened, and the girl who was wounded was not screaming in pain?"

"I did not hear anyone scream. I did not hear a noise, sir."

One commissioner pressed Ramirez about the blood. "One can only imagine the gore of the crime scene, which no doubt, had to have gotten all over you and your clothes."

"No, nothing was on my clothes."

"So a girl was at your feet, with her head blown off, and you got no blood on your clothes?"

"No, sir."

"Okay."

Only one commissioner had found an explanation for why Ramirez reloaded that seemed plausible to me. It was in a risk assessment letter written by an executive director of forensic evaluation and counseling services. He wrote, "Just as a child who has accidentally broken his toy may try in vain to put the shattered pieces back together, Mr. Ramirez was a drug-crazed immature teenager, who, in his stupor recklessly caused a catastrophe. In the instant Mr. Ramirez witnessed the destruction he had accidentally caused, in horror and shock he regressed to the level of a small child. He reloaded the weapon in an unconscious, pathetic attempt to fix what he had done, put the bullet back in the gun, to turn back the clock."

I believed that once Ramirez realized he couldn't turn back the clock, he blocked out the terrible carnage of the shotgun blast—the blood, the gore, the groaning screams of fear. He was in denial, protecting himself from the trauma of what he had done. That was why he didn't realize until the next day that someone had been killed. As with his plan for the robbery, instead of processing and reflecting, he kept moving toward an exit and flew to California the next day.

Thirty-three years later, Ramirez wanted to prove he had moved past who he was at that defining moment of his life. He quoted Norman Vincent Peale: "What he said was if you can change your thoughts you can change the world. And I've changed my thoughts. I no longer think like I'm an adolescent." He offered examples to prove that he understood what he had done and had changed. At one hearing he tried to equate his mother's diabetes and long-standing health issues to what his victims at the Burger King were feeling. "Because what she is suffering now, I can only imagine what the victims of my crime suffered that night and suffer lifelong because of my actions." The commissioner doesn't see the connection and admonishes him, saying, "Frankly, it's a stretch, Mr. Ramirez."

At a later parole hearing he told a more analogous story. While working as a shift manager at a White Castle, his mother was robbed at gunpoint. "I heard the panic, the frightened tremor in her voice," he said. "And I was scared. And I was afraid for her." Though he acknowledges that her suffering is nothing like a family losing their child, he felt that now "I know and I understand what the victims of my crime endured and had suffered."

At hearing after hearing, the parole board found Ramirez lacking and denied his parole. "You continue to offer dubious explanation of events to mitigate your actions." "Despite your lengthy incarceration, you have failed to conform your behavior as a civil and potentially law-abiding person otherwise would." And finally, "Your release would be incompatible with the welfare of society, and would so deprecate the serious nature of the crime as to undermine respect for the law."

But at the 2012 hearing, one commissioner disagreed and dissented from the decision to deny parole. Ramirez used his training as a legal clerk, in which he helped other prisoners with their appeals processes, to appeal the board's decision to deny his parole. Rather than gamble with a whole new set of commissioners, he wanted a do-over with at least one commissioner he knew to be sympathetic to his release. So began an appeals process that resulted in five years of postponements. He is accused of "commissioner shopping" and told, "You seem to be rescheduling this an awful lot." He's warned by the parole board that "we are not going to keep postponing this. This is nonsense to keep postponing this, when you know exactly what's going on." If remorse and regret weren't enough to get him out, he was going to get out on a legal loophole.

I was impressed but also wary of his ingenuity. Those legal aid jobs had paid off. I begrudged him his freedom. The more I learned about Ramirez, the more I realized I didn't want him to get out. I didn't think he deserved to be free. But there were plenty of people who did. He had numerous recommendations from people inside the facilities, as well as outside, who were able to overlook his crime and focus on the person he seemed to have become. There were black marks all over the page, concealing the names of the people vouching for Ramirez, most of them in law enforcement. One commissioner read what he described as "a very, very good letter on your behalf" from a prison chaplain who called Ramirez by his nickname, "Sandy," and who was proud to say their "close friendship" had escalated to a father-son relationship. There were recommendations from a number of corrections officers. Even a former chairman of the parole board had written a letter on his behalf that said he felt Ramirez would be able to "live a very productive life."

I thought about what my father had said, that the boys who killed Karen were young enough to still make something of their lives if they were released from prison. My father could've been one of those black marks, one of the many law enforcement personnel who had recommended that Ramirez be released. He could have written a letter on Ramirez's behalf—though I remembered him specifically saying he had gone to a parole board hearing for one of the boys. I could easily see my father showing up unannounced, barging in, determined to say his piece and have it included in the official record. Even though I never found proof of an in-person visit or a letter from my father, I believed he'd done something. My father had forgiven. I should have been able to.

I couldn't move past this. I knew the old saying about taking poison and waiting for the other person to die. I knew that withholding forgiveness would hurt only me. But I couldn't just force myself to move on because it was supposed to be better for me. It wasn't real forgiveness if the only reason I forgave was to benefit myself, because I wanted to feel better. Then I was no better than Ramirez, who seemed selfish and self-absorbed to the point of narcissism.

After years of counseling people deep in the process of forgiving, the Nobel Peace Prize winner and archbishop Desmond Tutu had observed that forgiveness involved four steps: acknowledging the harm, telling the story, granting forgiveness, and releasing the relationship. Maybe I couldn't forgive because I wasn't ready to release. I was holding on, stuck in what

I thought was the righteous anger of the wronged. Maybe forgiveness was about transcending anger and pain, having compassion for someone else as you would want for yourself. Or maybe it was even simpler than that.

Forgiveness meant letting go of the past. Moving on from an unattainable desire that the outcome could be different. Karen wasn't coming back. But even if the outcome couldn't change, the person responsible should. I didn't believe Santiago Ramirez had changed.

Maybe I was being too hard on Ramirez. Maybe I had read the transcripts with a black heart and a jaundiced eye. He said he wanted to atone, and maybe he had done everything he could to follow the rules. He was no longer a drug addict, no longer getting into trouble in prison. He said, "For me, remorse is something that has a lot of action. It's not just words, it's actions. And my actions are to tell me that I need to give back to the community in any way that I can so that I am actually empowering other people to enjoy their lives instead of taking them and causing destruction. So I think about my victims every day." I know he did, because when asked, he recited all the victims' names. It leaves black marks all over the transcripts. They could have blacked out the entire paragraph just of names, but someone went to the trouble of blacking out each name, first and last. He remembered the first *and* last name of every person in the Burger King that night. It was remarkable. Or it was a parlor trick meant to impress the commissioners.

At every hearing he talked about the robbery as "a decision that I truly regret" and said "I am remorseful for my actions." He made a point of always saying that he took "full responsibility for killing Karen." And clarified that it was not because he was caught, but "because it's not my place to take anybody else's life; and Karen Marsh had a promising life, and could have had a serious and significant effect on society as a whole." He was saying all the right things. But that was the problem.

During one hearing, Ramirez talked about what his high school English teacher had written in his senior yearbook: "It takes longer to get there when you take shortcuts." At the time he said he hadn't understood what the teacher was trying to tell him. Now he knew it meant that when you run from your problems, you're not dealing with them.

But I didn't believe Ramirez ever felt the true weight of taking Karen's life. It all felt parroted back from someone else telling him what he should feel, what he should say. The heat of the truth never radiated off him. He was not digging deep, exposing the bones buried underneath. He never submitted to the pain or succumbed to the deeper feelings that live beneath remorse and regret: shame and vulnerability. It was like after the shotgun went off, he wouldn't look closely at all. Everything he did in prison was about proving he could make it on the outside. To do that, he had to take control of the narrative of his life.

He lied to the parole board when he said he had never committed a crime before, something his codefendants eventually admitted in their own parole board hearings. He said his family didn't know why he went to California, when court documents show that he'd told his sister he had killed Karen and she'd helped him hide the shotgun in their apartment. Ramirez wanted to control the story about himself the way he had tried to control the robbery. He said he chose to carry the shotgun instead of the pistol because "I think the shotgun has the image effect of having more control." He admitted that "at that time I wasn't really thinking about letting somebody else take control."

Ramirez had a peculiar way of taking ownership of the victims of the crime by referring to them as "my victims." That phrasing made it clear that he was responsible, but it was also as if he still exercised some measure of control over them. I remembered something I'd read in the transcript from the sentencing hearing: he said he would not be a victim. He would be in control. He hadn't changed. He was still the angry young man feeling disrespected who asked, "What about my parents, what about me?"

When asked what was the most significant thing he had learned since being incarcerated, he answered, "That I learned how to forgive myself for taking Karen Marsh's life." He was even trying to take control of whether or not he was forgiven. This made my blood boil. The arrogance and nerve. The selfishness. I read his transcripts over and over. I even retyped the passages into topic areas to understand what really happened. Again and again Ramirez said he had regret, he had remorse, he took responsibility. But in ten parole hearings over the course of fourteen years he never once said the words "I'm sorry." He forgave himself, but he had never asked to be forgiven.

I didn't forgive him. I couldn't.

CHAPTER TWENTY-TWO

I spent the morning gathering all the paperwork I'd accumulated on Santiago Ramirez, including twelve years' worth of parole board hearing transcripts and a small stack of thin white business envelopes holding letters from Victim Assistance. The letters announced when his parole had been denied or his next hearing date was scheduled. As I put the letters in order, I realized that the three most recent ones were unopened. One of the envelopes had a green certified mail sticker across the front and back. It had been delivered even though the mail carrier hadn't bothered to get my signature. I sliced it open and expected another notice of postponement or denial, but the letter simply stated that Santiago Ramirez had been released. Parole had been granted. Stunned, my breath caught. He was out.

My body tensed under the weight of what felt like a brick on my heart. I realized I was still holding my breath and inhaled as deeply as I could manage. But the air was shallow in my lungs and just made me feel tighter, more out of breath, like a fish on land. Bubbles of oxygen stuck in the back of my throat, blocking the passageway. *Hard to swallow*, I thought, drowning in the news of Ramirez's release. I dropped my head into my hands and opened my mouth wide. Devastation washed over me. I wanted to curl into a ball, close my eyes, and make it all go away, or at least take time back to the moment right before, when I didn't know that he was free and all was lost.

How could a letter so small contain such big information? I was mad that they hadn't sent a larger packet, a manila envelope at least, something of a size proportional to the news contained therein. A visual warning that the contents would be heavy enough to break my spirit. The green certified mail sticker should have alerted me. I flared up with anger at my mail carrier for not getting my signature on the envelope. But really I was mad at myself for being so naive. I never thought Ramirez would actually get out. I thought he would die in prison. At least that's what I had hoped. And even though he had spent the last thirty-six years behind bars, it wasn't punishment enough. My father had been right: Ramirez was young enough to still have a full life. Karen never would. I was stung by the injustice of it, frustrated by how helpless I felt. There wasn't anything I could do to keep Karen's killer inside now.

My cousin Warren hadn't sent an email to let me know Ramirez was out. I hadn't told him that I'd added my name to the list of victims to be informed of Ramirez's status. I didn't want to seem like I was inserting myself into the situation or intruding on a painful, private matter. After Warren's initial request to send a letter to the parole board and a brief exchange of emails, we had not spoken about Karen again. We reverted to our private, solitary grief. The background buzz of lifelong mourning. Except for Christmas cards, we hadn't been in touch at all. I couldn't imagine what he and his family were going through.

But I easily imagined Ramirez's family celebrating the news. Screams of delight, hands clasped in front of quivering lips, eyes filling with tears of joy. The idea of their happiness angered, even offended me—though I guessed their happiness and joy were likely tinged with anger that their loved one had suffered, that he had stayed in as long as he had. They would say he was punished and had paid for his crime. For them, it was over. But for my family, the grief would never end.

I felt betrayed by the parole board, even though I understood that the commissioners weren't concerned with forgiveness. They wanted to know that the inmate had changed, that he could be a productive member of society. They wanted to mitigate the damage of letting criminals back on the street, to be assured that further crimes would not be committed. Forgiveness was not in their purview.

I was unsettled by the idea that Ramirez would no longer have to answer for killing Karen, no longer have to profess his regret and remorse, let alone prove it. Parole was the last stop before he would move on and disappear into the world with no one to answer to and no one keeping track of him.

I was sick to my stomach. I'd never sent the letter I'd written to the parole board, but I was mad at myself for not sending a letter against his release. I should have written to the parole board, letting them know that I had read all the transcripts and pieced together the truth: that Ramirez had not changed, that he was a liar. I needed to quell the negative emotions firing off inside me like faulty synapses. There was only one thing I could think of to do: I wanted to meet him. To see him with my own eyes. And for him to see me, to know that there were still people who would never forget what he had done. He may have forgiven himself, but he was unforgiven.

When I called Victim Assistance, I couldn't bring myself to ask about Ramirez. I was too angry, still smarting from the news of his release. I remembered that Francisco Alemar had told the parole board he wanted to say he was sorry to the family. I asked about getting in touch with him instead. The woman from Victim Assistance said inmates were not allowed to send letters of apology to their victims. It was too traumatic, like being revictimized. She said for the families, even receiving letters from Victim Assistance felt like an attack. She was right. That was exactly how I had felt opening the letters about Ramirez's parole: assaulted. She said that instead they offered a service called the Apology Program that allowed inmates to write letters to their victims that were then placed in their files. It was up to the victims to ask for the letters. I remembered reading that before he was sentenced, Torres had written a letter apologizing to Karen's parents, but the hearing judge was reluctant to pass it on. The woman from Victim Assistance put me on hold as she checked both Alemar's and Torres's files. But no letters had been left. She gave me the names and phone numbers for their parole officers. I pictured men like my father and "the guys from the job." Before I hung up, I asked for the contact info for Ramirez's parole officer as well.

The secretary for Ramirez's officer wanted to know if I was having trouble with the parolee. I assured her I was not and left a message for the officer to call me back.

I wasn't able to speak directly to Alemar's parole officer, either. His secretary told me that Alemar was no longer on parole. He had been released a year earlier and now was truly free. The secretary asked if I was okay leaving my phone number so that Alemar could contact me—if he wanted. I was thrown. I hadn't thought through how any of this would work. Under normal circumstances I might have been nervous about giving my personal information to a convicted murderer. I imagined her trying to fit all this onto the space of a pink message slip for the parole officer to explain to Alemar and suggested it would be better if I wrote it in a letter that could be passed on. The words came quickly and easily. "Dear Mr. Alemar," I began. I said I was Karen Marsh's cousin and that he shouldn't be anxious, I bore him no ill will. I explained that I had read in his parole board hearing transcripts that he had been discouraged from reaching out to Karen's family. If he was still willing, I wanted to meet him in person. I gave my phone number and email address and asked him to contact me. Unlike with writing a letter to the parole board about Ramirez, I didn't procrastinate. I mailed the letter that day.

I called to find out about Luis Torres. Unlike Alemar, Torres was still under parole supervision. That was not a good sign. He might have had a difficult time adjusting to life outside and gotten into trouble. I didn't know what to make of the fact that he was still in the town where he had been in prison. Perhaps he was in a halfway house, transitioning to life on the outside. I was curious about what had happened to him. But I didn't feel compelled to meet with him. I put the information about his parole officer aside.

Two weeks later I still hadn't heard back from Ramirez's parole officer. But I received an email from Frank Alemar. His thoughts were deeply personal. Once again, I was moved by his sincerity, how genuine his remorse was. He said he was living his life in memory of Karen Marsh. Overwhelmed by emotion, I shared what he had written with my sister but no one else in the family. I didn't want to violate his trust. I realized I didn't need to sit across from him. I didn't want to dredge up painful old feelings. I didn't need to ask what happened or have him tell me what I already knew from reading the transcripts. As I mulled over the idea of meeting with

Alemar, the unexpected happened—the tension inside me came undone. It loosened, then dissipated. I felt something that up until then I wasn't sure really existed: closure. I had the sense that my journey to understand the boys, now men, who had killed Karen was complete. Emailing Alemar was oddly soothing. His words comforted me. I felt satisfied and uplifted in a way I hadn't expected. He was a successful ex-convict. I was gratified that he had made it. It gave me hope to know that we could overcome the worst moments of our lives. Emailing Mr. Alemar also strengthened the connection I had to Karen and brought her to life in a way I hadn't felt before—because he and I didn't connect over her death, but what her memory, the fact of her existence, had sparked in our lives. Knowing that someone else was thinking about her warmed my heart and helped heal the wound.

My brief email exchange with Mr. Alemar made me question whether I really wanted to meet with Ramirez after all. Why did I want to sit across from him? What did I think I would get out of seeing him in the flesh? What did I want to ask? What did I have to say? Would meeting him make me change my mind and feel better about his being out on parole? What if meeting him only confirmed what I already suspected, that he should not be free? That he should die in prison? And now that he was free, why would he agree to meet with me, to be judged by me? What lies would I have to tell to convince him to meet with me? Would I have to say I wanted him to make something of his life, like Mr. Alemar, even though I didn't really care? I hoped he wouldn't hurt anyone else. He seemed troubled, but now he was on his own. Set adrift with his remorse and regret. Flotsam.

I was angry. And disappointed in myself for feeling that way.

I knew my anger would not go away easily. Maybe I did need to meet Ramirez. If I didn't, I would always wonder if meeting him could have helped me, made me feel better. At least if I met him I could say I tried everything to find forgiveness—the way Ramirez had forgiven himself. I realized that was the one question I wanted to ask: How? How had Ramirez overcome the shame, the guilt, of killing Karen?

How could I overcome the shame, the guilt, of beating up my father?

It's hard to forgive others when we don't forgive ourselves. When we can't admit that we have hurt others as badly as we have been hurt. So strong is our desire to think we are better that we don't admit when we are wrong, and therefore we deny ourselves the chance to actually become better.

When I attacked my father, I wasn't defending my mother, I was unleashing my own pent-up anger, rage even, at how he had controlled me. I wasn't a hero, I was an angry teenage girl lashing out. I had blocked the memory because I couldn't face what had happened. Defending my mother against a physical attack was a good thing. But using violence, especially against my father, went against everything I seemed to hold dear about myself as a good girl, a good student, a good daughter.

I had to take responsibility for my actions. To acknowledge and accept what I had done. I did what I had to do—seemed like a good idea at the time. *I beat up my father.* I felt remorse. I had regret. But I wasn't sorry. I forgave myself.

CHAPTER TWENTY-THREE

I wondered what my father would have thought about all this. I think he would have been proud that I'd looked deeper into parole and tried to follow his wishes. Although he might just as easily have chastised me for making contact with parolees. I still wanted his approval, even though he had been dead for over a decade. Thinking about parole for Karen's killers unearthed the unresolved anger I had buried about my father. I was unsettled that my enduring impression of him was framed by the worst of his actions—the physical abuse of my mother. But a person's true character is revealed during a crisis. I thought about the months leading up to my father's death.

I heard about how he acted up from my mother and sister. No doctor would see my father twice. He showed up to appointments loaded for bear. The doctors told him to stop smoking, that the cancer was progressing. My father disagreed, suggested they try again. Then he would reach into his jacket and pull out a gun, the old snub-nosed .38 with the homemade grip he'd fashioned out of rubber bands and duct tape.

Curbside at the airport, after a visit, I told him he couldn't keep threatening doctors because he didn't like the diagnosis. He looked annoyed, then his face darkened until I started to cry. He pulled me into a bear hug. *Get your house in order*, said the voice inside my head. Instead I pulled my bags behind me into the terminal, wiping away the tears. I flew back to LA and drank glasses of bad airplane red wine, looked out the window, and watched movies in the sky.

My mother and sister bore the brunt of his caregiving. I heard about it on the phone, long-distance in California. He pulled IVs out of his arms, cracked his head scrambling to climb out of the coffin-like MRI. He lunged at my sister in a crowded waiting room full of bald and dying cancer patients traumatized enough already by chemo. He raised a limp fist and threw punches that didn't land but hurt worse than if they had.

A few weeks earlier, another retired parole officer had died. He had cancer, too. So he took his old service revolver and stuck it into his mouth. His wife had cleaned his blood and brains off the wall. My sister made the trek out to Queens from Manhattan and helped my mother gather up my father's guns. My mother said she wouldn't let him be a family annihilator. He wasn't going to take her out, too. They found revolvers and automatics in shoeboxes, behind the World Book Encyclopedias, underneath the false bottom in a drawer. His weapons were hidden everywhere. When I got there, I found three more under the eaves in the attic next to bags full of our old stuffed animal toys—he couldn't bring himself to throw them away. We turned in the two guns that had paperwork, and I lingered over the third, hidden at the back of a closet that smelled like cedar, mothballs, and plastic-covered wool. It was a Smith & Wesson matte-black-handled .45 with a long silver barrel. It was handsome and dangerous, dark and shiny all at once. I shifted it back and forth in my palms, considering the weight, how it was both heavy and light. And until it was shot, unknowable.

My father was six feet, three inches tall. The next time I got out to Queens, he had shrunk to five foot eleven, 135 pounds.

When I walked into the bedroom, he sat up and reached for me. I could have wrapped my arms around him twice. I can't remember if he said my name or just the exhale of relief like an explosion from his diseased lungs. Then he sank down into the bed, exhausted from the effort. The rest of the day I expected him to sit up, to talk, to ask for a cigarette, but he didn't. He nodded or shook his head but never said another word. He winced when the nurse lifted him for a sponge bath and pulled his pajama bottoms down unceremoniously. He tried to cover himself with the sheet but she fussed his shaky hand away. I turned my head.

My father wouldn't eat. My mother said he was starving himself, taking control of his death the way he tried to control everything in life. I watched her hold up a cup of water with a straw to his lips but at an angle so awkward he could neither sip nor drink. *She's killing him*, I thought, snatching the cup away and giving him the first taste of water he might have had in days.

That night I sat with him. Holding his hand, stroking his arm. His breathing was labored. He wheezed in and out like a broken bagpipe. I considered the torturous road that lay ahead. I wanted to leave. To pat his hand three times reassuringly, then run. I couldn't take another minute, let alone another day, another week, another month.

I left and went downstairs. My mother sat in the living room with a distant cousin and her husband, who had come to visit. I spread out with supplies at the dining room table and wrote my father a note in big block letters with a black felt-tipped pen on a white sheet of paper—I LOVE YOU DADDY. I went upstairs to tape my message to the wall where he could see it. But he wasn't breathing anymore.

I stood over his birdlike body, back arched, hands curled like claws, mouth pulled into a rictus. He was so small. I wanted to cradle him in my arms, like a pietà. I felt his skin but he wasn't cold. Maybe he wasn't dead. I went downstairs and told my cousin's husband but not my mother, not yet. But the distant cousin wanted to be helpful and called 911. Next thing I knew, flashing lights were on the walls; I heard three steady, hard raps on the door.

The paramedics were first, then two cops in uniform who couldn't have been more than twenty years old. Seasoned detectives followed. They crossed the threshold, but I held them all at bay in the foyer. I didn't want them to go upstairs, to find him alive or, worse, to revive him. I was writing for *Law & Order*, stories about my father, I knew what would happen next. I thought of the mess: the broken ribs, the scattered latex gloves and bloody gauze. I knew my rights and I refused to let them see him. I said he was under hospice care, he had a DNR. They said that didn't matter, the call had been made and they needed to check on him. I knew that, too. I asked my mother for the DNR. She hemmed and hawed. I told her to hurry. She peeked inside a few drawers, then said she couldn't find it. But she pulled me aside and confessed—Daddy didn't have one. My father hadn't signed one. He wouldn't sign a paper that put control of his life in someone else's hands. But without that piece of paper they were going to go upstairs and bring my father back to life. If there was any life left in him. But I knew he wouldn't have wanted to live that way—brain-dead, most likely, broken ribs and broken spirit.

I called the technical consultant on the show, an assistant medical examiner for the City of New York. He called his boss. His boss called the police station. Within minutes everyone was gone. As they were leaving, I heard one of the young cops turn to his partner and ask, "Who was that old guy?"

He was a father, a husband, a son of a bitch—a man. Neither bad nor good, capable of both bad and good deeds.

My mother and I sat on both sides of him, telling stories over his dead body. Stories of the way he swam the butterfly in the ocean and that summer in Spain. Making my sister bedsheet fortresses in the backyard and sneaking me sips of whiskey sour at a bar. Stories of the way he always said "Love you, baby." The times he told me, "You did good." We didn't talk about when he hit her. Or when we'd hit him back.

"He was a good man." My mother kept saying it: "He was a good man."

He was a good man.

He was.

CHAPTER TWENTY-FOUR

The boys, now men, who had killed Karen were out of prison—on parole or free. I had made peace with that. I thought about going to visit Karen's grave at Valhalla. I had never been. But I realized I didn't want to go. I didn't want to see her final resting place, to acknowledge the end. Karen had been killed, but she had not died. She would always be alive inside me. Just like my father.

We buried his ashes at Woodlawn Cemetery in the Bronx. The first time I visited with my mother and sister, we couldn't find the plot. Woodlawn was more like a park than a graveyard. We wandered through the bucolic setting over green rolling hills on tree-lined paths, winding past the graves and grand mausoleums of American leaders, titans of industry, musicians, authors, and the humble headstones of everyday people. My father's grave was unmarked. The absence of a tombstone didn't signal neglect so much as indecision. We couldn't decide: Black marble or white stone? Chiseled with a lily of the valley or a weeping angel? Should we quote his favorite poem? Was he missed, devoted, or beloved? I was in no rush to complete this task. One more thing left to do meant there was one more reason to interact with his memory and temporarily bring him back to life.

When we found the plot, my sister and I sat in the overgrown grass on top of where we thought my father was buried.

Cross-legged, smiling in our sunglasses, we felt comforted to know where he was. My mother took a picture.

My father had never said he was sorry or asked for forgiveness for what he had done to my mother, for the trauma he had caused. I never asked or expected him to. My feelings about forgiving him were complicated. I was ashamed and embarrassed to admit this had happened in my family. I felt guilty, like I was somehow betraying him to even acknowledge what he had done. I knew my father would not have forgiven me for talking about it. I found myself wanting to mitigate and making excuses—like my mother when she would remind me it had happened only six times. But it *had* happened. Still, I couldn't reconcile the way my father had acted with my desire to protect his memory and reputation.

If I forgave him, it would be because I didn't want to dwell on the fact that he had done something wrong. I didn't know if forgiveness was even possible, since he was dead and couldn't ask for it himself. And it would have been hard for my father to admit what he had done, to acknowledge that he was someone who needed forgiveness, to put himself in the same category as parolees who had committed crimes like Alemar, Torres, and Ramirez. I was grateful to my cousin Warren for asking me to write a letter, for the process I'd gone through while considering their paroles. It wasn't lost on me that my father had forgiven them, too. Surely I could forgive my father. Then I realized that somehow, somewhere along the way, I already had.

ACKNOWLEDGMENTS

I started writing prose because I had grown weary of the scripts I wrote for television needing to be interpreted by other artists before the words could come to life. I wanted to create the product that in the end was completely mine. I have since learned that no creative endeavor is ever a completely solitary process—and actually the better for it. So I need to thank the many people who helped me start, muddle through the middle, and finish this book.

In the beginning there was Eric Simonoff, who, with Margaret Riley King, encouraged me to put pen to paper when this book was just an idea. Then Eric agreed to be my literary agent and made space for me on his roster when he wasn't taking on new clients. Eric's confidence in me and this work has meant everything.

I am so thankful to have found Sara Nelson, who has proved to be incisive, insightful, and everything I hoped for, wanted, and needed in an editor.

I would like to thank all the teachers I have had at UCLA Extension Writers' Program. First and foremost Erika Schickel, who taught me not only what a memoir was but also how to write one. This book would not exist without her. Thank you, Erika, from the bottom of my heart for all that you taught me in service of this craft.

I am indebted to the wisdom of Samantha Dunn, whom I first met at Cheryl Strayed's Esalen workshop, followed to classes at UCLA, and then to Boot Camp at Pam Houston's nonprofit Writing By Writers. Sam taught me how to write an essay as well as how to embrace the true meaning of the word "essay," from the French *essayer*, defined as "to try." The idea of trying, with its inherent permission to fail, was a freeing notion as I learned to write memoir.

Thank you to the Allegra Johnson Prize at UCLA for selecting me as a 2015 finalist for their very first memoir award. This bit of encouragement gave me the confidence to continue, and also introduced me to Jennie Nash, whose brutally honest critique of my early pages was just what I needed to drill down on what this memoir was really about.

I am forever grateful to the workshops that accepted me and helped me generate pages and further chapters: Sirenland, where I worked with Dani Shapiro, whose suggestion of reportage added a whole other dimension to the book; and the Cuba Writers Program, where I learned to keep the flame alive from the quiet passion of Tim Weed and Alden Jones. And thanks to fellow Sirenlander Katrina Woznicki, who introduced me to CWP and whose no-nonsense notes and attitude inspired me to keep going.

To Michael Connelly, Eric Overmyer, and Dan Pyne for running a tight enough ship on *Bosch* so that I could take time off to attend the writing workshops that became essential to my process.

To my colleague and friend, Tom Bernardo, who listened then talked me through a structural issue I didn't realize I had. His guidance and attention to detail led me to a path that landed at the deeper meaning in the narrative of my life.

Thank you to all my readers, classmates, and fellow workshop attendees for their close reading, notes, and encouragement over the years, in particular Matthew Lieberman, Rebbie Brassfield, Angela Featherstone, Sunita Puri, Gesa Buttner, Margareta Svensson Riggs, Verner Soler, and Henriette Ivanans.

I couldn't have crossed the finish line without Saba Saghafi and his thorough and exacting research into life's big questions and the small details of my childhood haunts.

I owe a debt of gratitude to the dedicated civil and public servants of the city at the New York State Department of Corrections and Community Supervision, Board of Parole, Office of Victim Assistance as well as to the Bronx DA Office Court Reporters, Bronx County Hall of Justice, and the Bronx County Clerk Office.

My love and appreciation to Barbara Marsh for her notes, corrections, and gracious support when I needed it most.

And, finally, thank you, Karen, for guiding me through it all.

ABOUT THE AUTHOR

Raised in Hollis, Queens, and educated at Harvard, ELLE JOHNSON got her first writing job on the television show *Homicide: Life on the Street*. Her credits include writing for series as varied as *Ghost Whisperer*, *Law & Order*, and *The Glades*, and co-showrunning Netflix's *Self Made: Inspired by the Life of Madam C. J. Walker*. She is currently an executive producer on the Amazon Prime series *Bosch* and has done everything from working in Egypt after graduation to studying screenwriting in the UK to riding a bicycle across the United States.